THE

COMICS

GUIDE TO
NEW YORK
CITY

D1538511

THE
MARVEL
COMICS

GUIDE TO
NEW YORK CITY

PETER SANDERSON

POCKET BOOKS
PUBLISHED BY SIMON & SCHUSTER
NEW YORK   TORONTO   SYDNEY   LONDON

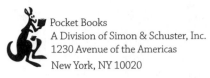
Pocket Books
A Division of Simon & Schuster, Inc.
1230 Avenue of the Americas
New York, NY 10020

Copyright © 2007 by Marvel Characters, Inc. All rights reserved.

MARVEL, all characters featured in this book and the distinctive likenesses thereof, and all related indicia, are ™ and © Marvel Characters, Inc. All rights reserved. www.marvel.com. Super Hero(s) and Super Villain(s) are co-owned registered trademarks. This publication is produced under license from Marvel Characters, Inc.

All rights reserved, including the right to reproduce this book or portions thereof in any form whatsoever. For information address Pocket Books Subsidiary Rights Department, 1230 Avenue of the Americas, New York, NY 10020

First Pocket Books trade paperback edition November 2007

POCKET and colophon are registered trademarks of Simon & Schuster, Inc.

For information about special discounts for bulk purchases, please contact Simon & Schuster Special Sales at 1-800-456-6798 or business@simonandschuster.com

Designed by Mary Austin Speaker

Manufactured in the United States of America

10   9   8   7   6   5   4   3   2   1

Library of Congress Cataloging-in-Publication Data

Sanderson, Peter.
The Marvel Comics guide to New York City / Peter Sanderson.—1st Pocket Books trade pbk. ed.
p. cm.
1. New York (N.Y.)—Tours. 2. New York (N.Y.)—Buildings, structures, etc.—Guidebooks. 3. Historic buildings—New York (State)—New York—Guidebooks. 4. Historic sites—New York (State)—New York—Guidebooks. 5. Literary landmarks—New York (State)—New York—Guidebooks. 6. New York (N.Y.)—In literature—Guidebooks. 7. Walking—New York (State)—New York—Guidebooks. 8. Marvel Comics Group—Miscellanea. 9. Comic strip characters—New York (State)—New York—Miscellanea. 10. Setting (Literature)—Guidebooks. I. Title.

F128.18.S258 2007

741.5'97471—dc22

2007023303

ISBN-13: 978-1-4165-3141-8

ISBN-10:   1-4165-3141-6

CONTENTS

vi

INTRODUCTION
"NEW YORK AND THE SUPER HEROES!"

FOR NEARLY SEVENTY YEARS Marvel Comics' writers and artists have chronicled the adventures of its Super Heroes in a fictional "Marvel Universe" that includes undiscovered lands and far-off galaxies. But the central focus, the true home, of this vast fictional cosmos is an all too real place: New York City. Peter Parker, alias the Amazing Spider-Man, was born and grew up in the borough of Queens; Steve Rogers, better known as Captain America, was born on Manhattan's Lower East Side. It is in Manhattan that two leading Super Hero teams, the Fantastic Four and the Avengers, are based.

Popular Marvel characters such as Peter Parker were not just born in New York City; they were created there, too. Marvel Comics' editorial offices have been located in Manhattan since the company's beginning, and New York City is not only where the American comic book business was founded, it remains the center of the comics industry today. Stan Lee, the editor and writer who co-created most of Marvel's classic heroes of the 1960s, was born in New York City; so was Jack Kirby, the artist who co-created Captain America, the Fantastic Four, the Hulk, the original X-Men, and many other members of the Marvel pantheon.

The forerunner of the comic book, the newspaper comic strip, also began in New York City. In the late nineteenth and early twentieth centuries, publishing moguls Joseph Pulitzer and William Randolph Hearst ran a variety of comic strips in an attempt to attract readers to their competing newspapers. Early-twentieth-century comic books were simply reprints of these newspaper strips. In the mid-1930s, however, the publishers began including original material as well. The Super Hero genre started in 1938 with the debut of DC Comics' Superman; the following year Timely Comics introduced the original Human Torch in *Marvel Comics* #1, the comic after which the company would rename itself in the 1960s.

For generations the traditional American hero in popular culture had been the frontiersman, or the cowboy: the man who brought justice to the untamed lands as the nation expanded westward. In contrast, the Super Hero was a pop-culture icon for a more modern, urban America, where the new frontiers lie in rapid, revolutionary scientific advances. As a result, the Super Hero is often an ordinary city dweller whom science endows with the abilities to make a difference in a city of millions.

It should be no surprise that the creators of the early Super Hero comics set their stories in urban centers that were similar to the New York City in which they lived and worked, and where many of them had been born and raised. It was the world they knew.

Thus, Superman was based in Metropolis; Batman defended Gotham City. Both were modeled on New York, but giving the city a fictional veneer removed the fantastic series even further from reality. They may as well have been set in the Neverland, or Middle-earth: no one could actually visit Gotham City or Metropolis.

Right from the start, however, Marvel was different. When the original Human Torch faced off with the Sub-Mariner in the 1940s, the battles were set in New York City.

But not until 1961 did longtime Marvel editor and head writer Stan Lee truly set a comic book revolution into motion. Assigned by his publisher to write a new Super Hero series, Lee was determined to show what Super Heroes would be like if they lived in the real world. He endowed them with multidimensional personalities and saddled them with realistic problems, ranging from troubles in love to making a living to contending against bigotry.

The first Super Heroes Stan Lee and artist Jack Kirby created were the Fantastic Four, who at first were based in Central City, a standard fictional name for a comic book metropolis.

Over at DC Comics, the Flash lived in a Central City, as had Will Eisner's The Spirit.

But by issue two Lee and Kirby decided to move the Fantastic Four to New York City, and by the issue after that, the FF were living in their new headquarters, which was not a Fortress of Solitude or Batcave, but an office building, which, by issue six, was referred to as the Baxter Building. The building is fictional, but apart from the unique modifications constructed by the Super Hero team on the upper floors, it is a typical, even nondescript Manhattan office building. Until Fantastic Four leader Reed Richards finally bought the Baxter Building outright, he had to worry about paying the rent and coping with Mr. Collins, the grouchy building manager.

This was all in keeping with Stan Lee's intentions for his Marvel revolution: if the heroes had real personalities and realistic problems in life, then they should live in a real city and work in a realistic place.

Marvel's main competitor, DC Comics, traditionally scattered its major Super Heroes in fictional cities around the country. Hence, Metropolis and Gotham City were somewhere in the Northeast, while the Flash's Central City was in the Midwest, and Green Lantern's Coast City was located somewhere on the West Coast. Bucking the trend, Stan Lee instead set almost all of his new Super Hero series in New York City. Even the Hulk, who spent most of his time out in the Southwestern desert, kept finding his way to New York. One benefit of this strategy is that it enabled Lee to easily have characters from one series cross over into another: for example, in *Amazing Spider-Man* #1 (March 1963) the title character visits the Baxter Building, hoping to find a job with the Fantastic Four.

But beyond just being based in the city, many Marvel Super Heroes were identified as true New Yorkers. Lee and his collaborators even went so far as to associate some of their characters with specific New York neighborhoods. Peter Parker, alias Spider-Man, grew up in the residential surroundings of Forest Hills, Queens, while Matt Murdock, the future Daredevil, was raised in a slum that writer/artist Frank Miller would later identify as Manhattan's Hell's Kitchen. Lee and

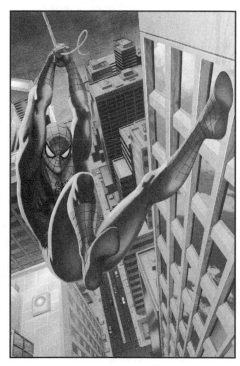

Kirby pitted Ben Grimm, the Fantastic Four's Thing, against the Yancy Street Gang, hinting at a connection between Ben and the Lower East Side neighborhood around the real-life Delancey Street.

Thus New York City became an integral part of "the Marvel Age of Comics."

Over the decades there have been attempts to move some of Marvel's core Super Heroes out of New York. In the 1970s Daredevil lived in San Francisco, and Thor was briefly based in Chicago in the 1980s. Following developments in the personal-computer business, Iron Man set up shop in Silicon Valley, California, in the 1980s and, more recently, in Seattle. For a decade the Avengers had a spin-off team, the West Coast Avengers, who operated out of Southern California. But all of these experiments eventually came to an end, and Marvel's leading Super Heroes have proved to be inseparable from the New York area. The farthest away from Manhattan that the core Super Heroes manage to get is the X-Men's mansion in New York state's Westchester County, only a short commute away.

Director Sam Raimi clearly recognized the importance of New York City to Marvel Comics, filming large portions of *Spider-Man, Spider-Man 2,* and *Spider-Man 3* on location in New York City, from Peter Parker's home in Queens to the sky-scrapers of Manhattan. In 2007, New York City mayor Michael Bloomberg acknowledged New York's role in the films by declaring the week of *Spider-Man 3*'s opening "Spider-Man in New York Week." There were events all over the city, from the premier of *Spider-Man 3* in Queens, to exhibits and events at the New York Public Library, the American Museum of Natural History, Rockefeller Center, and the Central Park Zoo—all of which have appeared in Marvel comics and films. The catch-phrase for Spider-Man Week was "A Hero Comes Home," which was precisely correct.

In this book we have attempted to list the major landmarks, both real and imagined, in Marvel's New York and describe how they have figured in Marvel history.

There are three classes of locations in Marvel's New York City. First, there are the sites that exist in the real world: Central Park, Madison Square Garden, the Empire State Building.

Then there are entirely fictional places supposedly located within the city, such as the Baxter Building. In a few cases Marvel has specified a street location for such imaginary sites, but more often these locales are simply mentioned as being in Manhattan, without further details.

The third category consists of fictional buildings, institutions, and places that are based on real-life counterparts. Among these are Avengers Mansion, which was inspired by the Fifth Avenue mansion of art collector Henry Clay Frick, and the Super Villain prison on Ryker's Island, a thinly disguised version of the actual Rikers Island facility for real-world criminals.

This guidebook is organized by neighborhood, in the hopes Marvel fans will be able to customize their own walking tours of New York City, visiting the settings of both famous and relatively obscure stories from Marvel's long, rich history. Long-time Marvel readers may well recall still more stories set at these locations that we did not have the room to include in this book. In the case of real places and institutions, we have included their real-life histories and descriptions to inspire readers to visit New York's many splendid tourist attractions on their own merits, not simply their comics connections.

As Marvel aficionados walk around New York, they are invited to imagine themselves touring its Marvel Universe counterpart, hoping to catch a glimpse of Spider-Man swinging by on his webbing, or the Fantastic Four zooming down Forty-second Street, headed for adventure.

Then again—would

you really want to live in the Marvel Comics version of New York City? After all, battles in Manhattan's streets between Super Heroes and Super Villains must happen weekly, or even daily!

Worse, catastrophes have repeatedly struck the entire island of Manhattan. New York considers itself "the capital of the world," and the headquarters of the United Nations is located there. Perhaps that is why the undersea kingdom of Atlantis makes New York its prime target in its war on the surface world. In 1941, Namor the Sub-Mariner, Prince of Atlantis, created an immense tidal wave that flooded Manhattan Island (as recounted in *Marvels* #1, January 1994). During the Sub-Mariner's initial encounter with the Fantastic Four, he used the Horn of Proteus to summon Giganto, a gargantuan, whalelike creature from the deep, which then rampaged through the city (*Fantastic Four* #4, 1962). Shortly thereafter, Namor directed an Atlantean invasion of New York (*Fantastic Four Annual* #1, 1963), which was thwarted by Reed Richards of the Fantastic Four. But the Atlanteans successfully invaded the city on subsequent occasions, as in *Sub-Mariner* #21 (January 1970) and in the "Atlantis Attacks" story line in Marvel's 1989 summer annuals.

The Atlanteans are not the only ones who have proved capable of taking Manhattan hostage. Aries, the head of the astrologically themed crime syndicate Zodiac, once headed up a mercenary army that captured Manhattan, wrecking all of its bridges in order to isolate it from the rest of the world (*Avengers*, vol. 1, #82, November 1970). Backed up by an army of gigantic Sentinel robots, the entity called Onslaught took control of Manhattan years later in 1996's "Onslaught Saga," which ran various Marvel titles, concluding with Onslaught's defeat in Central Park in *Onslaught: Marvel Universe*.

But at least these menaces left New York City where they found it. The Nazi war criminal called the Red Skull once captured Manhattan Island within a gigantic bubble and levitated it into the sky (*Tales of Suspense* #90, June 1967). You might think that this was a once-in-a-lifetime event, but you would be wrong. The alien marauder Terrax likewise levitated Manhattan into orbit around the Earth in order to blackmail the Fantastic Four into battling his master, Galactus, for him (*Fantastic Four*, vol. 1, #242–43, May–June 1982).

Believe it or not, that was not the strangest fate to befall Manhattan. The ancient sorcerer Kulan Gath once cast a spell that temporarily transformed Manhattan into a city from the prehistoric age of Conan the Barbarian (*Uncanny X-Men* #190–91, February–March 1985)!

Taking all that into consideration, why haven't the denizens of Marvel's Manhattan packed up and moved out? Another

Marvel character, Patsy Walker, once provided the answer. She was the star of her own long-running comic for young girls, beginning in the 1940s. After her own series ended, Patsy turned up in a Super Hero series, *Avengers,* and in issue 144 (February 1976) she explained why she had left her small-town home: "New York and the Super Heroes!" By the end of that issue, she became a Super Heroine herself, known as Hellcat.

Here writer Steve Englehart had hit upon a reason for the connection between Super Heroes and New York City. For generations young people, and not-so-young people, have migrated to New York to start their careers, to find fame and fortune, and even to remold their identities, not unlike Patsy did in donning her Hellcat costume. It's why immigrants, such as the parents of the first generation of Super Hero comics creators, traditonally come and settle in New York City. This city has a reputation of being larger-than-life, almost magical, a place where anything can happen, where a virtual nobody can remake himself into a success on a national scale.

Super Heroes fit this mythic image of New York. Marvel's New York is literally full of marvels. The Super Hero represents the potential within every individual to become extraordinary. What better setting could there be than New York, where people flock every year in the hopes of making their dreams come true? ✳

CITY HALL

City Hall Park
Broadway at Park Row

NEW YORK CITY HALL is the site of the mayor's office and the chambers of the City Council.

Built between 1803 and 1812, New York City Hall is the oldest still-functioning city hall building in the United States and a National Historic Landmark. (There were two previous city halls in Manhattan. The second, still standing in the Wall Street area, is today known as Federal Hall.) Its architects, John McComb Jr. and Joseph François Mangin, designed the exterior in French Renaissance style, and the interior in the American Georgian style.

Peter Parker and Mary Jane Watson were married on the steps of City Hall by her uncle, Judge Spencer Watson, both in the comic books (*Amazing Spider-Man Annual* #21, 1987) and simultaneously in the *Amazing Spider-Man* newspaper strip.

Though this was arguably the most memorable event in Marvel history to take place at City Hall, it is by no means the only one.

In the movie *Spider-Man 2,* after Spider-Man rescues his aunt May in a death- defying struggle with Doctor Octopus, he leaves her in front of City Hall.

Back in the 1940s, Captain America and Bucky confronted the Reaper, a demagogue who secretly served Adolf Hitler, at City Hall (*Captain America Comics* #22, January 1943). Captain America pursued the Reaper into a nearby subway station, where the Nazi agent was electrocuted by the third rail.

Decades later, Jonathan Darque, the supercriminal known as Magma, threatened to use his "tremor inducer" to trigger

an earthquake in New York. Magma then publicly appeared at City Hall to deliver an ultimatum to the city, but was attacked in front of the building by Iron Man. Magma activated his tremor inducer, but Spider-Man manipulated the machine with his webbing, diverting the tremor away from the city and out into the Atlantic Ocean (*Marvel Team-Up* #110, October 1981). ✳

TIMELY PLAZA

JENNIFER WALTERS LEADS A dual career as the green-skinned Super Heroine, the She-Hulk, and as one of Manhattan's leading attorneys. She is currently employed by Goodman, Lieber, Kurtzberg & Holliway, a firm that specializes in legal cases involving Super Heroes and Super Villains. Their offices are at Timely Plaza, which She-Hulk writer Dan Slott has suggested is located near the New York City Supreme Court buildings on Centre Street. This places Timely Plaza somewhere between Canal Street to the north and City Hall to the south.

Timely Plaza is, of course, named after Marvel Comics' original name, Timely Publications. But the name of Jennifer's law firm is also in part an homage to Marvel history. Martin Goodman was Marvel's original publisher and founder. Stan Lee and Jack Kirby, the co-creators of Fantastic Four, the Incredible Hulk, and other Marvel series, were born Stanley Lieber and Jacob Kurtzberg. Holliway, however, is simply the last name of Holden Holliway, the GLK&H senior partner who hired Jennifer (and who first appeared in *She-Hulk* #1, May 2004), and does not appear to be an homage to anyone. ✳

WORLD TRADE CENTER/GROUND ZERO

FOR THREE DECADES THE Twin Towers of the World Trade Center, the tallest buildings in Manhattan at 110 stories, were iconic symbols of New York City. The Twin Towers were known throughout the world as physical representations of America's economic might, and that symbolism made them a target. In the real world in 1993, terrorists set off explosives in the underground garage of the North Tower, in an attempt to topple the North Tower into the South Tower, leveling both buildings. On that occasion the terrorists failed. But on September 11, 2001, terrorist hijackers flew two planes into the towers, causing them to collapse. The five other buildings at the site were so severely damaged that they had to be demolished. Nearly three thousand people perished in this horrific catastrophe. The site of the devastation is now known as Ground Zero.

It was corporate mogul David Rockefeller who first conceived of the World Trade Center. Whereas most headquarters of major businesses were located in midtown, Rockefeller proposed locating the World Trade Center in lower Manhattan, to stimulate economic development there and so that it would be close to Wall Street, home of the New York Stock Exchange.

The Twin Towers were designed in modernist style by architect Minoru Yamasaki. The North Tower, known as 1 World

Trade Center, was completed in 1970, and the South Tower, 2 World Trade Center, was opened for occupancy in 1972. Not only was each building taller than the Empire State Building, but the Twin Towers were briefly the two tallest buildings in the entire world. They lost the record in 1973 to Chicago's Sears Tower, (although, if you include the North Tower's antenna, 1 World Trade Center was still higher by 1.9 feet!).

The principal occupants of the Twin Towers were financial firms and government organizations. The celebrated restaurant Windows of the World resided on the 107th floor of the North Tower. Visitors to the South Tower could take elevators up to the 107th indoor observation deck, affording astounding views of the city and its harbor, or even go up to the roof itself. Roughly fifty thousand people worked each day in the Twin Towers. In fact, the Towers contained so much office space that they had their own zip code, 10048.

The rebuilding of the World Trade Center, including the new Freedom Tower and a "transportation hub" for underground trains, is currently under way, with an estimated completion time of 2011.

In Marvel history before 2001, the World Trade Center played a less prominent role than one might now expect. But some stories now seem eerily portentous of the real-life disaster that was to come.

5

After climbing the Statue of Liberty, the gigantic alien Gog looked for the highest point in the city. He sighted the newly completed World Trade Center towers and teleported himself atop one of them. From there Gog teleported himself again to an unrevealed location (*Astonishing Tales* #18, June 1973).

The astrologically themed criminal cartel Zodiac threatened to utilize their Star-Blazer weapon to murder everyone in Manhattan who had been born under the sign of Gemini. Like Gog, Zodiac sought the highest point overlooking Manhattan and set up the Star-Blazer atop one of the World Trade Center towers. Following the same logic, the Avengers found them there and crippled their weapon. Zodiac member Aries threw the Avengers' ally Mantis over the roof of one of the Twin Towers. While the Avengers rescued her, Zodiac made their escape (*Avengers,* vol. 1, #120–21, February–March 1974).

The jaded hedonists of the Gotham Game Club decided to have a competition among themselves to kill the Hulk when he next surfaced in New York City. One of the gamesmen, Peter Niven, was a stockbroker whose offices were located in the World Trade Center. At the World Trade Center site, Niven fired laser weapons at the Hulk from within an airborne helicopter. The Hulk brought down the helicopter, but Niven bailed out safely (*Incredible Hulk Annual* #9, 1980).

Shang-Chi, the Master of Kung Fu, battled his father Fu

Manchu's bionic servant Maru atop one of the World Trade Center towers. Finally, Shang-Chi kicked Maru off the top of the tower to his death (*Master of King Fu* #88, May 1980).

The nearly omnipotent entity Galactus transformed the alien tyrant Tyros into his cosmically powered herald, Terrax the Tamer. But Terrax rebelled and fled to Earth in order to compel the Fantastic Four to join him in destroying his master. Galactus caught up with Terrax and divested him of his cosmic abilities, causing Terrax to fall from the top of one of the World Trade Center towers. Far luckier than Maru, the superhuman Terrax amazingly survived the fall, although, not surprisingly, he was gravely injured (*Fantastic Four,* vol. 1, #243, June 1982).

One of the powerful multinational corporations that had offices in the World Trade Center was Roxxon Oil, which conducted covert illegal operations. One of Roxxon's vice presidents, Jerry Jaxon, held a meeting in his World Trade Center office with various superhumans who were former trainees of the Canadian government. Jaxon organized them into the criminal team known as Omega Flight, who subsequently battled the Canadian Super Hero team Alpha Flight at the World Trade Center. In the melee Jaxon was seemingly killed through electrocution (*Alpha Flight,* vol. 1, #11–12, June–July 1984).

The "demons of Zor" briefly made their base at the World

Trade Center, which they transformed into the Weird Trade Center, until Zor was driven off by the Vision, the Scarlet Witch, Quicksilver, and Power Man (*The Vision and the Scarlet Witch* #8, May 1986).

The Irish mutant criminal Black Tom Cassidy and his partner, the virtually unstoppable Juggernaut, invaded a business meeting at the World Trade Center and took the participants hostage as part of an attempt to forcibly stop a corporate takeover. Spider-Man and the mutant strike force X-Force came to the rescue. Cassidy set off explosives, which did not, however, inflict major damage on the Towers. X-Force leader Cable shot Cassidy, who fell from one of the Towers, but was rescued by the mercenary Deadpool (*X-Force* #1–5, August–December 1991).

A mentally unstable costumed vigilante who called himself the Master of Vengeance decided to impersonate Spider-Man, even forcing a former friend, Vicary, to create gloves that enabled the Master to duplicate Spider-Man's wall-crawling ability. With the drugged Vicary in tow, the Master, disguised as Spider-Man, climbed up one of the World Trade Center towers. When the real Spider-Man showed up, the Master hurled Vicary toward the ground. The same trick that had worked for Aries worked for the Master as well: as Spider-Man attempted to save Vicary, the Master of Vengeance made his escape (*Spider-Man,* vol. 1, #32–34, March–May 1993).

In a possible reference to the actual 1993 terror attack, an armored criminal named Terror Unlimited held the World Trade Center hostage, until he was defeated by Spider-Man and his cloned counterpart, the Scarlet Spider (*Spider-Man Unlimited,* vol. 1, #8, February 1995).

The Hulk's archenemy, the Leader, once secretly controlled a terrorist organization called the Alliance. In an even more explicit allusion to the 1993 terrorist attack, the Leader planted one of his artificially created Humanoids in the underground garage of the World Trade Center, where it exploded (*Incredible Hulk,* vol. 2, #439, March 1996; *Avengers,* vol. 1, #397, April 1996).

General Cecil B. Slinkard was a founding member of Control, a military advisory council that monitored superhuman activity. Following the collapse of Control, Slinkard was mysteriously set on fire and fell from the top of one of the World Trade Center towers. Although his death was called a suicide, Slinkard was reportedly connected with subversives and may have been murdered (*Conspiracy* #2, March 1998).

Following the 9/11 attacks, Marvel released *Amazing Spider-Man,* vol. 2, #36 (2001), an issue with a solidly black cover, in which the title character visits Ground Zero and reflects on the tragedy. Other Super Heroes are shown helping to clear away the rubble, and even Doctor Doom and Magneto show up to pay tribute to the fallen.

Additionally, Marvel published *Heroes,* a sixty-four-page collection of single-page illustrations paying tribute to the firefighters, police officers, medical workers, and others who tried to save people—and in many cases died themselves—on September 11. The proceeds from the sale of the comic went to charities that helped those who were suffering in the aftermath of the attacks. Among the more memorable images from

this issue is that of a grieving Captain America looming over the Manhattan cityscape, as smoke pours from the ruins of Ground Zero. Marvel also published an anthology of comics stories about the attacks, titled *A Moment of Silence.* ✳

ALICIA MASTERS'S STUDIO

THE MOST UNUSUAL ARTIST in Marvel's New York is Alicia Masters, the girlfriend of Ben Grimm, the Thing of the Fantastic Four. Despite her blindness, Alicia has become a successful sculptress, specializing in iconic, life-size images of the Fantastic Four and other "Marvels." Her studio and home are in TriBeCa, the "triangle below Canal Street," in lower Manhattan.

In Stan Lee and Jack Kirby's great "Galactus Trilogy," the alien Silver Surfer battled the Fantastic Four at the Baxter Building in midtown. The Thing struck the Surfer so hard that he crash-landed in Alicia's TriBeCa studio. There she persuaded the Surfer to rebel against his master, Galactus, in order to protect humanity (*Fantastic Four*, vol. 1, #48–50, March–May 1966).

TriBeCa was also the location of the headquarters of the original X-Factor, an organization founded by Professor Charles Xavier's first class of mutant students: Cyclops, Marvel Girl, Angel, Beast, and Iceman (*X-Factor* #1, February 1986). ✳

187 CHRYSTIE STREET
Between Stanton and Rivington Streets

SOUTH OF HOUSTON STREET, Second Avenue becomes Chrystie Street, which was named after Lieutenant Colonel John Chrystie, a hero of the War of 1812 and a graduate of Columbia University.

Number 187 stands across from Sara Delano Roosevelt Park, which was named after the mother of Franklin Delano Roosevelt, the former president and governor of New York State. The park, which spans from Houston Street to Canal Street, is home to various sports facilities, including a basketball court.

Number 187 Chrystie Street was used for the exterior shots of Peter Parker's apartment building in the movie *Spider-Man 2* (2004). But the filmmakers may have intended Peter's apartment to actually be located in the uptown Morningside Heights area, inasmuch as Mary Jane Watson later runs from that neighborhood's Riverside Church to Peter's apartment building.

Though Peter's apartment looks low-rent in the movie, 187 Chrystie Street actually houses various upscale stores and boutiques. ✳

DELANCEY STREET/YANCY STREET

READERS OF FANTASTIC FOUR know Yancy Street as the home of the Yancy Street Gang, a pack of pranksters who continually play practical jokes on Ben Grimm, the Thing. In the real world there is no Yancy Street, but there is a Delancey Street on Manhattan's Lower East Side, which was presumably its inspiration. After all, Jack Kirby, the co-creator of the Fantastic Four, was born in 1917 on Suffolk Street, in the Delancey Street neighborhood.

In the early decades of the twentieth century, Delancey Street and Houston Street (pronounced "how-ston," unlike the city in Texas) bordered a section of Manhattan that was primarily populated by European Jewish immigrants and their families. Most of the people there were poor and lived in cramped apartments in tenements. Kirby's teenage years coincided with the Great Depression.

Such harsh conditions spawned the growth of gangs. At one end of the spectrum were the criminal organizations run by legendary mobsters "Lucky" Luciano, Meyer Lansky, and "Bugsy" Siegel. At the other end were gangs of teenagers who banded together to play games and to fight with rival gangs from nearby neighborhoods. Kirby belonged to one of the latter sort, the Suffolk Street Gang, and despite his being short was reputedly a pugnacious fighter.

The criminal gangs and teen gangs of the Lower East Side inspired plays and movies and television shows over the decades. In its 1935 Broadway production, Sidney Kingsley's play *Dead End* featured a group of young actors who reappeared in the 1937 movie version and became known as the Dead End Kids. They subsequently turned up in the Warner Bros. gangster movie *Angels with Dirty Faces,* opposite James Cagney, who grew up on the Lower East Side, and went on to star in a long-running series of comedies as the East Side Kids and the Bowery Boys. These likable young roughnecks were surely a primary influence on Stan Lee and Jack Kirby's Yancy Street Gang.

The Yancy Streeters were first mentioned in *Fantastic Four* #11 (February 1963) and were first glimpsed in issue 15 (June 1963). (Oddly, issue 15 indicates that Yancy Street intersects Tenth Avenue, which would put it on the West Side. This is most likely an error.) For decades their faces were never shown in the comics, nor was it revealed just why they kept pulling pranks on the Thing. Despite their peripheral role in *Fantastic Four,* Lee and Kirby were obviously fond of them, and the story in issue 29 (August 1964) was even titled "It Started on Yancy Street."

In *The Thing* #1 (July 1983) writer John Byrne finally brought the gang members out into the open and revealed the Thing's connection with them. According to this story, Ben Grimm was born on Yancy Street. His older brother, Daniel, was the leader of the Yancy Street gang, who were at that time a band of hoodlums. When Ben was only eight, Daniel was killed in a fight between the Yancy Streeters and a rival gang. Ben joined the Yancy Street Gang and eventually became its new leader. However, Ben's uncle Jake, who was a doctor, prevailed on him to leave the gang and enter high school, setting him on the road to becoming a pilot and a member of the Fantastic Four.

The other Yancy Street Gang members also went straight when they grew up, and many seem to have become construction workers. It seems that they harassed the Thing out of a mix of resentment that he'd left them behind and affection for their old friend. Indeed, from time to time the Yancy Street Gang have aided the Thing and the rest of the Fantastic Four against their enemies.

A new Yancy Street Gang, a multiethnic "kid gang" who are decidedly not criminals, first appeared in "Miracle on Yancy Street!" in *Fantastic Four* #361 (February 1992).

The Golem of Yancy Street,

known as Joseph, was an artificial being that was created to protect the Jewish people from oppression. Transported to the United States by his creator, Joseph was buried beneath a building on Yancy Street, but awoke when the building was demolished. The Thing subsequently battled the Golem, which now lies inert in the East River (*Marvel Knights,* vol. 4, #22, November 2005).

In the Marvel Universe, Stan Lee was recently bicycling down Yancy Street when he ran into the Thing. Lee asked the Thing how his feud with the Yancy Street Gang started, and the Thing blamed it all on Stan for writing about it. Lee had long portrayed the monstrous Thing as a tragic figure and declared he would write a story in which the Thing finally returned to human form. But as Stan watched, Ben Grimm single-handedly captured a group of bank robbers and basked in the adoring attention of female spectators. Then Ben told Stan that he didn't want to be human again, because his life had turned out pretty well, after all (*Stan Lee Meets the Thing* #1, December 2006). ✳

THE BOWERY

AT THE END OF the eighteenth century, the Bowery was the address for many of Manhattan's wealthiest residents. But their mansions gave way to flophouses by the middle of the nineteenth century, and by the Great Depression of the 1930s, the Bowery had become New York City's most infamous slum.

The Bowery is a small neighborhood, bounded by the East Village to the north, the Lower East Side to the east, Chinatown to the south, and Little Italy on the west. In recent years the neighborhood has been revitalized and is probably best known as the location of the now defunct CBGB's.

But it was the Bowery's notorious reputation as the haunt of alcoholic derelicts that must have inspired its foremost role in Marvel history. Having angrily quit the Fantastic Four, Johnny Storm, the teenage Human Torch, wandered into a Bowery flophouse, where he found an old 1940s comic book featuring Namor the Sub-Mariner, the prince of undersea Atlantis. There Johnny also encountered an amnesiac homeless man with long, shaggy hair and a beard, who demonstrated unusual strength. Recognizing him, Johnny used his flame power to burn away the man's beard and excess hair, revealing him to be the Sub-Mariner himself. The Torch then flew Namor up into the air and dropped him into the East River. The trick worked, and the shock reawakened Namor's long-lost memories (*Fantastic Four,* vol. 1, #4, May 1962).

Various other Marvel characters who hit low points in their lives eventually found themselves on the Bowery.

Another 1940s Super Hero, the original Whizzer, was driven by depression to alcoholism and spent months living as a derelict on the Bowery.

The original Ant-Man's archenemy, Egghead, has repeatedly hidden out from his enemies in the Bowery, starting with the end of his first appearance in *Tales to Astonish,* vol. 1, #38 (December 1962).

The criminal surgeon Dr. Jonas Harrow found a hit man for the criminal syndicate called the Maggia (which operates out of nearby Little Italy) lying in a Bowery alley, left to die with his skull shattered. Harrow replaced the damaged portion of the man's skull with steel, and the hit man became the gang boss called Hammerhead (*Amazing Spider-Man,* vol. 1, #114, November 1972).

Even Doctor Strange's mentor, the Ancient One, was once reduced to the level of a drunken homeless man living in the Bowery by the evil sorcerers known as the Creators (*Doctor Strange,* vol. 2, #26, December 1977).

As stated earlier, the Bowery has undergone considerable rejuvenation in recent years. In fact, Johnny Storm was amazed to discover that the flophouse where he had first encountered the Sub-Mariner had later been converted into an off-off-Broadway theater (*Fantastic Four,* vol. 1, #242, May 1982). The play being performed there was a stage adaptation of Wendy and Richard Pini's comic series *Elfquest,* which was once published by Marvel's Epic line. ✳

THE COFFEE BEAN/ COFFEE A GO GO

LONG BEFORE THE RISE of Starbucks, young people socialized in Greenwich Village coffeehouses in the 1950s and early 1960s. The coffeehouses were hangouts for members of the "Beat generation," a movement that included such literary figures as poet Allen Ginsberg, a New Yorker. During this period many coffeehouses provided live entertainment, most notably folk singing and poetry readings.

Since so many classic Marvel series started in the 1960s, it should be no surprise that the coffeehouse phenomenon was an element of the characters, social lives.

Peter Parker (alias Spider-Man), Mary Jane Watson, and their friends frequented the Coffee Bean, a student hangout in the East Village near their college, Empire State University. Created by Stan Lee and John Romita, the Coffee Bean first appeared in *Amazing Spider-Man* #53 (October 1967). On the evidence of 1960s Spider-Man comics, the Coffee Bean was a rather tame place, especially compared to its competition over in the *X-Men* comics.

On their trips into Manhattan in their everyday identities, the original X-Men—Cyclops, Marvel Girl, Angel, Beast, and Iceman—headed for the Coffee a Go Go, which was Stan Lee and Jack Kirby's affectionate parody of a beatnik coffeehouse of the early 1960s. Its star attraction was Bernard the Poet, the Marvel version of Allen Ginsberg or Lawrence Ferlinghetti, complete with goatee. In the Coffee a Go Go's first appearance (*X-Men*, vol. 1, #7, September 1964), Bernard declaimed his poems to the customers while female modern dancers performed interpretative dances. The X-Men seemed bewildered but amused.

Maybe the X-Men liked the place because the beatniks appreaciated nonconformists. On their first visit, Henry McCoy, the Beast (before he grew his blue fur), said his feet hurt and removed his shoes. Amazed by the enormous size of his mutant feet, the beatnik crowd hailed McCoy as unique and carried him on their shoulders as a hero.

In fact, the X-Men liked the Coffee a Go Go so much that they even held a birthday party there for Bobby Drake (Iceman), and Bernard composed a special poem for the occasion (*X-Men,* vol. 1, #32, May 1967).

THE COFFEE BEAN/COFFEE A GO GO

21

THE COFFEE BEAN/COFFEE A GO GO

By this time Bobby was dating one of the Coffee a Go Go's waitresses, Zelda (whose last name remains unrevealed). The exact location of the Coffee a Go Go in Greenwich Village was never specified. However, in 2000 writer/artist John Byrne drew the apartment that Zelda shared with the Beast's girlfriend, Vera Cantor (*X-Men: The Hidden Years* #2, January 2000). A fan of the TV series *Friends*, Byrne made the building look like Monica and Rachel's apartment. So perhaps Vera and Zelda lived in the same building that *Friends* used for exterior shots, 90 Bedford Street, on the corner of Grove Street in the West Village.

Coffee shops have remained a part of Village life, on well-known streets such as MacDougal Street, Bleecker Street, and Christopher Street, and in recent years coffee shops have resurged in popularity. This may be why Doctor Strange has nowadays magically disguised his Greenwich Village town house as a Starbucks under construction.

ANTHOLOGY FILM ARCHIVES
32 Second Avenue (at Second Street)

ANTHOLOGY FILM ARCHIVES IS a nonprofit institution dedicated to the study, preservation, and exhibition of avant-garde and experimental films. Originally based at Joseph Papp's Public Theater, where it opened in 1970, Anthology Film Archives eventually bought and moved into the Second Avenue Courthouse building. Today this building houses two theaters, which show not only American independent films but also classic foreign films. The building includes a library, a gallery, a film-preservation center, and an archive holding around eleven thousand films.

In the movie *Spider-Man 2* (2004), the Anthology Film Archives building houses Dr. Otto Octavius's laboratory, where he demonstrates his fusion reactor to the press. Octavius also shows off his metal harness containing robotic tentacles that respond to his mental commands, which he uses to manipulate dangerously radioactive materials. But his demonstration goes awry when a nuclear accident fuses the harness to his body. As a result Dr. Octavius goes insane and becomes the Super Villain Doctor Octopus.

DOCTOR STRANGE'S SANCTUM SANCTORUM
177A Bleecker Street

GREENWICH VILLAGE HAS A long-standing reputation as the home of nonconformists and even eccentrics. In the Marvel Universe, one of these unconventional residents is Dr. Stephen Strange, who lives in an impressive three-story town house, #177A, on one of the West Village's best-known streets, Bleecker Street. The house, known as his Sanctum Sanctorum, first appeared in Doctor Strange's debut story in *Strange Tales* #110 (July 1963).

In the late 1960s, new Marvel writers Roy Thomas and Gary Friedrich shared an apartment at the real 177A Bleecker Street. Thomas, one of the leading writers in Doctor Strange's history, subsequently decided to give the same address to the doctor's town house.

Strange was once a famous and wealthy surgeon, until his hands were damaged in an automobile accident. He lost his fortune and even became an alcoholic derelict, until he left New York for an expedition to Tibet.

On his return, Strange took up residence in this Bleecker Street town house and became known as a self-styled expert on the occult. The majority of people laughed at his claims, but some individuals ventured to 177A Bleecker Street to seek his help. Doctor Strange was indeed a "Master of the Mystic Arts," who eventually became the Sorcerer Supreme of Earth.

From the outside, Strange's town house looks distinguished but not particularly distinctive, except for the unusual design of the window serving as a skylight for the topmost floor.

Once he enters, however, the visitor may notice that the house is somehow much larger inside than it appears to be from the outside. In fact, it is not known just how many rooms the house contains. Moreover, the layout of the house's interior seems to change magically from time to time (accounting for the lack of consistent depictions in the comics).

Some features of the interior, however, remain consistent. The basement is used for mundane purposes, such as storage and laundry, and contains the furnace. The living and dining rooms and library are on the first floor, and the second floor holds separate bedrooms for Strange, his assistant Wong, and any guests.

It is the third floor that is most properly described as Dr. Strange's Sanctum Sanctorum. Here he keeps his mystical artifacts and objects of power. The most important of these, the Orb

of Agamotto, is housed in its own chamber. The third floor also contains Strange's meditation room and his library of occult volumes, most notably the Book of the Vishanti. From this topmost floor, Strange conducts his mystical research and rituals.

The site on which Strange's house was built is a focal point for magical energies. Native Americans conducted mystical rituals there in the centuries before the coming of the European settlers. Reportedly, pagan rites of some unknown sort were held there as well. It has not been revealed who built the town house on the site, or when, or who occupied it before Strange acquired the property. It is known that before Strange moved in, people considered the house to be haunted. Doctor Strange modified the house to suit his purposes, doubtlessly in large part by magical means.

Doctor Strange's house long served as a headquarters for a loosely knit Super Hero team called the Defenders, who met in the first-floor living room and library. Currently the house serves as headquarters for the New Avengers, the team to which Strange now belongs.

For years Doctor Strange welcomed visitors who sought his aid in combating magical dangers. Strange had created a permanent spell of mystical force, connecting with the house's own occult energies, to shield it from magical attack.

Recently, however, Doctor Strange has with a mystical spell camouflaged his house as a building being converted into a Starbucks coffee shop. The Doctor does not often thus demonstrate his sense of humor. ✳

JOE'S PIZZA
233 Bleecker Street at Carmine Street

AT THE START OF the movie *Spider-Man 2* (2004), Peter Parker has a job delivering pizzas at the Joe's Pizza on Bleecker Street. In the movie this pizza shop has a policy that if they're late delivering the pizza, the customer doesn't have to pay for it. Unfortunately, Peter Parker keeps being diverted from his delivery duties by going into action as Spider-Man. He tries web-slinging from the rooftops to get a pizza delivered in time, but finally his boss gives him the boot.

In real life Peter wouldn't have kept the job even if he had always made the deliveries on schedule. Due to rent increases, owner Joe Pozzuoli closed his Bleecker Street store in 2004, after the movie was filmed. But Pozzuoli still operates another Joe's Pizza nearby at 7 Carmine Street. ✳

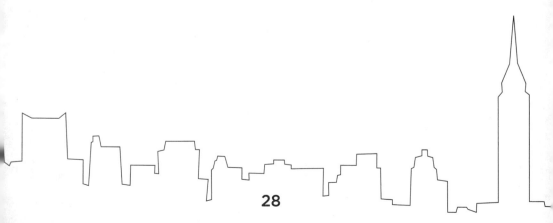

MOONDANCE DINER
80 Sixth Avenue at Grand Street

ONE OF MANHATTAN'S HANDFUL of surviving vintage diners, the Moondance Diner dates back to the 1930s, although the distinctive sign featuring a revolving moon is less than twenty years old. The diner is open from 7 a.m. to midnight, seven days a week.

In the movie *Spider-Man 2,* aspiring actress Mary Jane Watson emerges from the diner only to run into her neighbor and high school classmate Peter Parker. Embarrassed to be working there as a waitress, Mary Jane tries to conceal her job from Peter, but the truth comes out when her boss calls after her.

Mary Jane is not the only pop culture character who worked at the Moondance. The situation comedy *Friends* portrayed the Moondance as a 1950s theme restaurant, and Monica ended up working there as a waitress in a costume including a blond wig and roller skates.

A real-life waiter at the Moondance was Jonathan Larson, the late composer of the Broadway rock musical *Rent.*

The diner is currently in talks to move to Wyoming, however, and by the time this book goes to press, may have already done so. ✻

NEW YORK UNIVERSITY/
EMPIRE STATE UNIVERSITY

BEFORE MARVEL REVOLUTIONIZED SUPER HERO comics in the 1960s, comic book characters rarely seemed to age. Readers might well have expected that Peter Parker, alias Spider-Man, would remain a student at Midtown High School forever. But in *Amazing Spider-Man* #31 (December 1965), scripter Stan Lee and artist Steve Ditko surprised their audience when Peter started his freshman year at New York City's fictional Empire State University. His Midtown High classmate "Flash" Thompson likewise became an ESU freshman. At ESU, Peter met other students who would play major roles in his life: his first true love, Gwen Stacy, and his best friend, Harry Osborn, who later became the second Green Goblin.

Peter eventually graduated from ESU and started graduate studies there. He has even taught courses there as an ESU teaching assistant.

Since there is no Empire State University in the real New York City, where did Marvel locate what appears to be its extensive campus?

Marvel's map of Manhattan, first published in *The Official Handbook of the Marvel Universe* in the 1980s, places ESU in the same location in Greenwich Village as New York University's main campus, near Washington Square Park. Moreover, the two names, Empire State University and New York University, and their initials, clearly resemble each other. So it appears that ESU was intended to be a fictionalized version of NYU. In the Chamber miniseries (October 2002–January 2003), the title character, who has enrolled at ESU, even lives in Brittany Hall, the name of an actual dormitory at NYU (at 55 East Tenth Street).

The real New York University was founded in 1831 and has grown to become the largest nonprofit educational institution in the United States. Its unofficial "quad" is Washington Square Park, best known for its distinctive Washington Arch, erected in 1885 to commemorate the centennial of George Washington's inauguration.

Famous NYU alumni include filmmakers Woody Allen, Ang Lee (director of the first *Hulk* movie), Spike Lee, Martin Scorsese, and Oliver Stone; actors Alec Baldwin, Billy Crystal, Whoopi Goldberg, Ethan Hawke, Philip Seymour Hoffman, Bryce Dallas Howard (who played Gwen Stacy in the movie *Spider-Man 3*), Felicity Huffman, Angelina Jolie, Burt Lancaster, and Adam Sandler; playwrights Tony Kushner and Neil Simon; novelists Joseph Heller, Frank McCourt, and J. D. Salinger; and legendary New York mayor Fiorello La Guardia.

Similarly, Marvel's Empire State University also has a stellar list of alumni. Past ESU students include Vance Astrovik (the Super Hero Justice), Hector Ayala (the White Tiger), Robert Farrell (the Rocket Racer), Emma Frost (the White Queen), Maria de Guadalupe Santiago (Silverclaw of the Avengers), Felicia Hardy (the Black Cat), Chip Martin (the superhuman menace called the Schizoid Man), Norman Osborn (the original Green Goblin), Richard Rider (the Super Hero Nova), Sarah Rushman (Marrow of the X-Men), Greg Salinger (the second vigilante known as the Foolkiller), Gwen Stacy's cousin Jill, Jonathan Starsmore (Chamber of Generation X), and Phil Urich (a heroic version of the Green Goblin). Mary Jane Watson-Parker, Johnny Storm (the Human Torch), and Brian Braddock (Captain Britain) all studied at ESU.

Besides several of Peter Parker's friends, a number of Spider-Man's enemies were teachers or administrators at ESU. Peter's mentor Dr. Curt Connors has repeatedly morphed into his enemy, the reptilian Lizard. Professor Miles Warren utilized his expertise in cloning as the nefarious Jackal. Professor Clifton Shallot became the third Vulture. ESU vice chancellor Edward Lansky turned to crime as the Super Villain Lightmaster. Professor Buck Mitty employs his expertise in entomology, the study of insects, as the costumed criminal Humbug. Drama professor Harrison Turk was actually an other-dimensional alien named Arisen Tyrk, who had an insane doppelgänger called Lunatik, who clashed with the Defenders.

Another notable ESU faculty member was biochemistry professor Ted Sallis, who later transformed into the mindless swamp monster called the Man-Thing.

The Fantastic Four's Reed Richards and Ben Grimm—and briefly the future Doctor Doom—attended an institution known as State University (*Fantastic Four* Annual #2, 1964). Lately there have been attempts to identify State University as Empire State University. However, in *Fantastic Four* #35 (February 1965), Reed Richards revisits State University, and it is clearly not in New York City. In the 1980s, *The Official Handbook of the Marvel Universe* established that State University was in Hegeman, a town apparently in upstate New York.

In the *Spider-Man* movies, Peter Parker attends neither ESU nor NYU, but Columbia University. ✳

FLATIRON BUILDING
Intersection of East Twenty-third Street, Broadway, and Fifth Avenue

A NATIONAL HISTORIC LANDMARK, the Flatiron Building is renowned for its unusual triangular shape, designed by architect Daniel Burnham. Its construction was completed in 1902, making it the second-oldest skyscraper in Manhattan. Originally officially known as the Fuller Building, the Flatiron Building gained its nickname from its resemblance to the irons used at the turn of the century. The name stuck, and the entire surrounding area is now known as the Flatiron District. The twenty-two-story building stands 285 feet tall and today houses numerous publishing companies.

In the *Spider-Man* movies, the Flatiron Building is the home of the *Daily Bugle*, the tabloid newspaper published by J. Jonah Jameson. In the comics, however, the *Daily Bugle* offices are located farther uptown.

In the Marvel Comics Universe the Flatiron Building is the site of the offices of Damage Control Inc., a construction and engineering firm that specializes in the repair and reconstruction of buildings damaged during battles between Super Heroes and their adversaries. (Damage Control was first seen in *Marvel Comics Presents* #19, 1989.)

Spider-Man once battled Doctor Octopus at the Flatiron Building (*Deadline* #2, July 2002). The Flatiron Building was also the base of Olivier, a demon who is an enemy of the Punisher (*The Punisher,* vol. 4, #2, December 1998). ✳

FLATIRON BUILDING

DAILY BUGLE BUILDING
East Thirty-ninth Street and Second Avenue

THE DAILY BUGLE IS a leading tabloid newspaper in Marvel's version of New York City, similar to the real-life *New York Post* and *New York Daily News*. Its owner and publisher is J. Jonah Jameson, who has been using the *Bugle* as a platform for attacking Spider-Man as a public nuisance ever since both he and his paper were introduced in **Amazing Spider-Man** #1 (March 1963). Ironically, the *Bugle* is famous for its exclu-

sive pictures of Spider-Man and other costumed characters, most of which were taken by freelance photographer Peter Parker, who is Spider-Man himself. (In the alternate continuity of the **Ultimate Spider-Man** series, Peter Parker is the *Daily Bugle*'s webmaster, not a photographer.)

Founded in 1897, the *Daily Bugle* was bought decades later by entrepreneur William Walter Goodman. As a result, the forty-six-story building housing the *Bugle* offices, at Thirty-ninth Street and Second Avenue, became known as the Goodman Building.

Daily Bugle photojournalist Phil Sheldon spent his long career covering Super Heroes since the debut of the original Human Torch in 1939 (*Marvels* #1–4, January–April 1994). As if foreshadowing Peter Parker's later role at the paper, *Bugle* reporter Jeff Mace led a secret life as the World War II Super Hero known as the Patriot.

One of Sheldon's colleagues at the *Bugle*, Walter "Old Man" Jameson, was the newspaper's publisher by 1945. Although he was no relation, the young J. Jonah Jameson regarded Walter Jameson as a role model, even adopting his mustache and flattop hairstyle. Starting when he was in high school, Jonah became a copyboy for the *Bugle* and worked his way up to become a reporter and then editor.

The *Bugle* was in financial decline when J. Jonah Jameson used his considerable inheritance to buy the paper. As publisher, Jameson turned the *Bugle* into a success and eventually purchased the Goodman Building as well. Jameson renamed the building after his paper, and thirty-foot-tall letters spelling out DAILY BUGLE currently stand atop the building's roof. From this headquarters J. Jonah Jameson Inc. has also published *Now* magazine and the defunct *Woman* magazine, edited by Carol Danvers. Recently Jameson also published *The Pulse*, devoted specifically to covering Super Heroes.

Jameson is infamous for attacking Spider-Man as a criminal menace in his headlines and editorials. However, apart from this obsession, Jameson has led an admirable career, using his paper to crusade for civil rights and to campaign against organized crime.

Jameson's right-hand man is *Bugle* editor in chief Joe "Robbie" Robertson, whose wisdom moderates his boss's excesses. It takes nerves of steel to deal daily with the volatile Jameson. Betty Brant had the endurance to serve as Jameson's secretary until she advanced to the position of one of the paper's top reporters; she was eventually succeeded as secretary by the equally strong-minded Glory Grant. Other significant *Bugle* reporters have included Daredevil's confidant Ben Urich, former Super Hero Jessica Jones, Betty's late husband Ned Leeds, and a reformed gangster, the deceased Frederick Foswell.

The *Daily Bugle* has had many ups and downs in its history, including its long-running competition with another (fictitious) New York tabloid, the *Daily Globe*. The *Bugle* was briefly owned at different times by Thomas Fireheart (alias the Puma) and Norman Osborn (the Green Goblin), but Jameson always reclaimed ownership.

Even though Jameson hates Spider-Man, the web-slinger has repeatedly found himself battling his costumed enemies at the *Bugle* offices. In fact, Graviton and the Green Goblin each wrecked the entire building on separate occasions, but the edifice was rebuilt each time.

Whereas the comics place the *Daily Bugle* building in the Murray Hill neighborhood, close to midtown, the **Spider-Man** movies have turned the Flatiron Building on Twenty-third Street, one of the city's earliest skyscrapers, into the site of the *Daily Bugle* offices. Jameson, Brant, and Robertson all appear in the movies. In **Spider-Man 3** (2007), reporter Eddie Brock, who becomes the Super Villain Venom, also works at the *Bugle,* whereas in the comics he reported for the *Globe.* ✳

DAILY BUGLE BUILDING

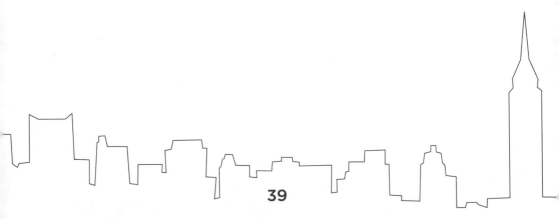

666 FIFTH AVENUE
Between Fifty-second and Fifty-third Streets

ORIGINALLY KNOWN AS THE Tishman Building, 666 Fifth Avenue is a forty-one-story office building erected in 1957 between Fifty-second and Fifty-third Streets. Sculptor Isamu Noguchi designed the waterfall fountain and the elevator-bank floors in the building's lobby. The building's largest tenant is currently the financial-services giant Citigroup.

In the Bible's book of Revelation, 666 is the number of the Beast. That may explain why, in 2002, the building's owners replaced the large, red 666 numbers from the building's facade with the logo CITI for Citigroup.

But Marvel writer Doug Moench had already seized the opportunity to set a satanic cult, the Left-Hand Path, at the top of the 666 building. (In actuality, the top floor then housed the Top of the Sixes restaurant.)

The cult's leader, Schuyler Belial, alias Morning Star, concocted a scheme to capture Jack Russell, the Werewolf by Night, so that Belial and his cultists could drink the Werewolf's blood and thereby supposedly gain the powers of the Beast. The cultists captured both Russell and his ally, the costumed vigilante Moon Knight, and took them to Belial's office on the top floor of 666 Fifth Avenue. Moon Knight and Russell escaped, but subsequently returned to 666 Fifth Avenue to battle the cultists. The Werewolf hurled Belial from the roof of the building to his death. (*Moon Knight,* vol. 1, #29, March 1983, and #30, April 1983.) ✳

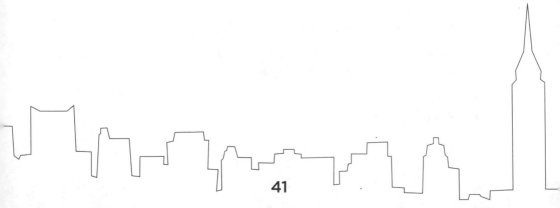

BAXTER BUILDING/FOUR FREEDOMS PLAZA
Forty-second Street and Madison Avenue

IN ALL OF MARVEL Manhattan, the building that is most closely identified with Super Heroes is the Baxter Building, the home and headquarters of the first modern Super Hero team, the Fantastic Four.

This fictional building is in a prime real-life location, along Forty-second Street between Grand Central Station (on Park Avenue) and the New York Public Library's main building (on Fifth Avenue).

According to Marvel history, the Baxter Building was constructed in 1949 by its original owners, the Leland Baxter Paper Company. It was originally an office building, thirty-five stories tall.

The Baxter Building first appeared in *Fantastic Four* #3 (March 1962). The Fantastic Four began their careers as Super Heroes in the fictional location of Central City, California. When they moved to New York City, they bought the top five floors of the building, although later, due to financial pressures, they sold the floors back to the owner and rented them instead.

Reed Richards, the leader of the Fantastic Four, undertook radical renovations of the top five floors. He even succeeded in obtaining legal permission to use the Baxter Building for launching aerial vehicles, notably the flying Fantasti-Car and "pogo plane." In fact, along one side of the Baxter Building Richards constructed a rocket silo, extending the length of the five-floor headquarters. The rocket's exhaust was transmitted safely through pipes down the side of the building and underground into the East River. Special materials in the silo's walls muffled vibrations from launching the rocket; presumably Richards eventually lined the walls with vibranium, the metal that absorbs vibration.

Since the Baxter Building was well-known as the Fantastic Four's headquarters, it became a target for their many enemies. In an attempt to destroy the team, Doctor Doom levitated the entire building into outer space (*Fantastic Four*, vol. 1, #6, September 1962). The Fantastic Four managed to return themselves and the Baxter Building to its proper site on Earth. But Doom later

recaptured the Baxter Building, and this time turned it into a base from which to attack the FF in the streets of Manhattan (*Fantastic Four*, vol. 1, #39–40, June–July 1965). Shortly after the Fantastic Four recovered their headquarters, the gargantuan "devourer of Worlds," Galactus, landed his spacecraft atop the Baxter Building, spreading panic throughout the world (*Fantastic Four,* vol. 1, #48–50, March–May 1966).

Despite Richards's security systems, Super Villains were continually breaking into the Baxter Building's upper floors to attack the Fantastic Four. After Galactus's former herald Terrax obliterated the top three floors, the FF's long-suffering landlord, Mr. Collins, finally decided to evict his troublesome tenants. But the Fantastic Four were in such good financial shape at that point that Richards simply purchased the building outright (*Fantastic Four,* vol. 1, #244, July 1982).

Nevertheless, the FF lost their home soon afterward when Doctor Doom's adopted son, Kristoff, deciding to improve on the master's old scheme, not only levitated the Baxter Building into space again but blew it up to boot (*Fantastic Four,* vol. 1, #278, May 1985).

The Fantastic Four survived and constructed a new headquarters, Four Freedoms Plaza, on the site of the former Baxter Building. This hundred-story building was named after the "four freedoms" in a famous speech by President Franklin D.

Roosevelt: freedom of speech, freedom of worship, freedom from want, and freedom from fear. The lower fifty floors were occupied by various tenants (including Wendell Vaughn, alias the Super Hero Quasar), while the FF's headquarters took up the top fifty floors.

During an extended absence of the Fantastic Four from Earth, however, a group calling themselves the Masters of Evil took over Four Freedoms Plaza and ultimately destroyed it. Finding themselves homeless upon their return, the FF moved into a New York waterfront warehouse, which they named Pier 4. This new base, in turn, was wrecked by their longtime adversary Diablo.

However, Richards and an inventor friend, coincidentally named Noah Baxter, constructed a new Baxter Building in outer space. Richards then teleported it to the site of the original Baxter Building, and it became the Fantastic Four's current headquarters.

Visitors to the Baxter Building will first encounter Sergius O'Hoolihan, the FF's loyal, longtime doorman. If they're lucky, they may also run into Willie Lumpkin, the semiretired mailman (played by Stan Lee himself in the first *Fantastic Four* movie) who continues to deliver the FF's fan mail. Tourists can easily persuade Mr. Lumpkin to demonstrate his own "superpower": his ability to wiggle his ears.

BAXTER BUILDING/FOUR FREEDOMS PLAZA

The Baxter Building's ground floor consists primarily of a visitors' center, including a Fantastic Four museum and gift shop. There is also a multimedia show celebrating the careers of the Fantastic Four, shown continuously between 9 a.m. and 4 p.m.

Various commercial tenants are also on the first floor. A while back, four Marvel monsters—Elektro, Googam, Gorilla, and the notorious Fin Fang Foom—were reduced to human size and given jobs at the Baxter Building. Fin Fang Foom became a chef at the Green Wok, a Chinese restaurant on the first floor, and Googam became a parking valet (*Marvel Monsters: Fin Fang Four* #1, December 2005).

An express elevator from the first floor transports the Fantastic Four to their headquarters on the uppermost floors. Only the FF can use this elevator, activating it with signals from devices in their belt buckles.

The following description of the Fantastic Four's headquarters floors is based on the assumption that the current Baxter Building has the same layout as the original.

Visitors with appointments to see the Fantastic Four must take one of the regular elevators to the reception area on the thirtieth floor. Seated behind a reception desk is the FF's receptionist, Roberta, who appears (from the waist up) to be a young blond woman, but is actually a robot. (She has dated another robot, Elektro, who works in the mail room.) The reception area contains hidden security devices, which administer electrical shocks to any visitor who proves to be a threat. Otherwise the thirtieth floor serves as a "buffer zone" to insulate the tenants below from any damage from battles with Super Villains that may occur on the Fantastic Four's floors.

The Fantastic Four's living quarters are on the thirty-first floor, including the dining room, bedrooms, and guest rooms. The library, medical facilities, and exercise rooms are on the thirty-second floor. The thirty-third floor holds Reed Richards's laboratories and includes the portal to the Negative Zone, an alternate dimension. The conference room, computers, and communication center are all on the thirty-fourth floor. The thirty-fifth floor is a large hangar for the Fantasti-Car and other

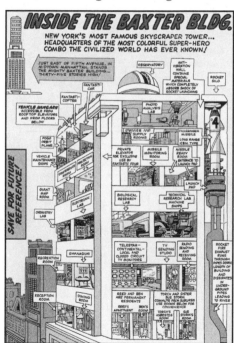

flying vehicles, which enter and exit through a hatch in the roof. Atop the roof is Richards's astronomical observatory, which presumably has advanced means of seeing past the pollution and round-the-clock electric lights of midtown Manhattan. *

CHRYSLER BUILDING

405 Lexington Avenue at East Forty-second Street

A MASTERPIECE OF ART deco architecture, the Chrysler Building is the second-tallest sky-scraper in Manhattan. Prior to the Empire State Building's completion in 1931, the Chrysler Building was the tallest building in the entire world. Built between 1928 and 1930, the building was designed by architect William Van Alen for the Chrysler Corpotation, and many of its architectural details are based on features of the company's cars. For example, the building's eagle sculptures resemble hood ornaments on Chrysler automobiles of the period. It is largely considered to be one of the most beautiful skyscrapers in the world.

In the movie *Fantastic Four: Rise of the Silver Surfer* (2007), the Human Torch pursues the Silver Surfer over the Manhattan skyline to the Chrysler Building.

A powerful punch from the alien Super-Skrull once catapulted the Thing onto the top of the Chrysler Building (*Fantastic Four,* vol. 1, #18, September 1963). History repeated itself when another menace, Abraxas, used his powers to propel the Thing through the air to collide against the Chrysler Building (*Fantastic Four*, vol. 3, #49, January 2002).

But perhaps the oddest appearance of the Chrysler Building in Fantastic Four history involves a talking ape called Gorr the Golden Gorilla. Gorr is one of the New Men, who are animals endowed with human-level intelligence by the High Evolutionary, a master of advanced genetic engineering. The High Evolutionary dispatched Gorr to Earth to contact the Fantastic Four. But when Gorr arrived, he mutated into a giant, ran amok in New York City, and even climbed to the top of the Chrysler Building (all in writer Roy Thomas's homage to King Kong). The Invisible Woman finally enveloped Gorr in her force field, thereby somehow causing him to revert to his normal size (*Fantastic Four,* vol. 1, #171, June 1976).

A mentally disturbed costumed man called the Trixter once climbed to the top of the Chrysler Building, claiming he could make it snow for Christmas. Once up there, he was struck dead by a bolt of lightning, but, ironically, it did then begin to snow (*Daredevil,* vol. 1, #241, April 1987).

The cyborg called Postmortem, who was an ally of Dracula's and an enemy of the vampire hunter Blade's, maintained a laboratory on the thirteenth floor (where else?) of the Chrysler Building for decades until his death (*Blade the Vampire Hunter*, vol. 1, #10, April 1995). ✳

CHRYSLER BUILDING

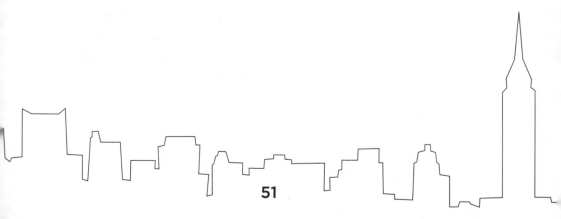

EMPIRE STATE BUILDING
350 Fifth Avenue between Thirty-third and Thirty-fourth Streets

THE TALLEST SKYSCRAPER in Manhattan, the Empire State Building is the most iconic symbol of New York City, widely recognized throughout the world. Its name comes from the nickname for New York State as the Empire State. The building is a masterwork of art deco architecture, and the American Society of Civil Engineers named it one of the Seven Wonders of the Modern World.

The Empire State Building stands 102 stories high, and its spire extends it farther to 1,454 feet into the sky. When the building opened in 1931, it was the tallest building in the world. The Empire State Building retained this record for four decades, until the construction of the World Trade Center's North Tower in 1972. Following the destruction of the World Trade Center's Twin Towers, the Empire State Building is again the tallest building in New York City, and the second tallest in the United States (exceeded by the Sears Tower in Chicago).

Observation decks, open to visitors, are on the 86th and 102nd floors.

At the top of the building are transmission facilities for virtually all of the radio and television broadcast stations in the New York City area.

In popular culture the Empire State Building is most famous as the setting for the climax of the original *King Kong,* which premiered only two years after the opening of the building.

The Empire State Building also played a special role in Marvel's real-life history. From 1942 to 1951, Timely Comics, the company now known as Marvel, was based on the building's fourteenth floor.

It should therefore be no surprise that the Empire State Building has figured prominently in various Marvel stories over the years.

For example, an immense alien creature called Klaatu, which resembled a whale and was as big as a skyscraper, once came to New York City, drawn by the city's enormous electrical power. Rendering itself immaterial, Klaatu entered the Empire State Building to feed on energy from the New York City power grid, causing a widespread power shortage. An alien named Xeron the Star-Slayer attempted to use his energy harpoon against the creature, but the Hulk interfered by attacking Klaatu, who soon returned to outer space (*Incredible Hulk,* vol. 2, #136, February 1971).

The exorcist Gabriel, Devil Hunter, maintained an office in the Empire State Building on (of course) its thirteenth floor (*Haunt of Horror* #2, 1974).

The Mandrill and his terrorist organization Black Spectre attacked the Empire State Building in a effort to cripple radio and television broadcasting, but were opposed by Daredevil and the Black Widow (*Daredevil,* vol. 1, #111, July 1974).

Shang-Chi, Marvel's Master of Kung Fu, is the son of the infamous Asian genius Dr. Fu Manchu. As part of his campaign to conquer the world, Fu Manchu attempted to install an antenna atop the Empire State Building, with which he intended to mesmerize the American populace through television broadcasts. Shang-Chi, Spider-Man, and Sir Denis Nayland Smith (Fu Manchu's nemesis from the original pulp novels) joined forces to foil the mastermind's plot (*Giant-Size Spider-Man* #1, October 1974).

A Super Villain called the Modular Man and his ally Killer Shrike stole a "molecular condenser" device that needed to be powered by microwaves. They then flew a helicopter over the Empire State Building, intending to use microwaves from its television antenna to power the device. It worked, and the condenser caused the Modular Man to increase in size and power. He raved that the process would transform him into a being of pure energy. The Beast and Spider-Man ruined the Modular

Man's scheme by firing a bolt of electricity at him (*Marvel Team-Up* #90, February 1980).

Charles Reigel, a member of the Gotham Game Club, proposed a competition among its members to kill the Hulk. After all the other members failed, Bruce Banner, the Hulk's human identity, confronted Reigel in his office in the Empire State Building. When Reigel attempted to shoot him, Banner transformed into the Hulk. Reigel then sent robots, designed to resemble chess pieces, to attack the Hulk, but the Green Goliath easily overcame them, and Reigel was taken into police custody (*Incredible Hulk Annual* #9, 1980).

After being transformed into a superhumanly strong creature called the Armadillo, Antonio Rodriguez found employment as a superpowered wrestler. When he found out that his wife had been cheating on him, the Armadillo went berserk and climbed up the Empire State Building, planning to kill himself. Captain America tried to change his mind, but the Armadillo leapt from the building. Amazingly, the superhuman Armadillo survived the fall, though he was seriously injured (*Captain America,* vol. 1, #316, April 1986).

During a battle between the mutant team X-Factor and their enemy Apocalypse aboard the Super Villain's flying headquarters, the ship struck the Empire State Building, causing the building's antenna to fall off (*X-Factor* #25, February 1988).

After the battle, the members of X-Factor repaired the damage to the building (*X-Factor Annual* #3, 1988).

But far worse soon followed. In Marvel's "Inferno" story line, the demon N'astirh planned to invade Manhattan by leading his fellow demons from the limbo dimension through a portal above the Empire State Building. The building transformed, becoming alien, even demonic, in appearance. Attempting to halt the invasion, Kang the Conqueror sent his size-changing android, the Growing Man, to attack the Empire State Building and the demons (*Avengers,* vol. 1, #300, February 1989). The mutant sorceress Illyana Rasputin sealed the portal, trapping the demons in limbo (*New Mutants* #73, March 1989).

Madelyne Pryor, a clone of Jean Grey who married Scott Summers (Cyclops) and bore him a son named Nathan, had become N'astirh's superpowered ally, the malevolent Goblin Queen. N'astirh and Pryor plotted to sacrifice the life of the infant Nathan in order to create a spell that would permanently open the portal between Manhattan and the limbo dimension. Pryor transformed the top of the Empire State Building into an altar and prepared to perform the rite. Then one of the members of X-Factor, Iceman, used his powers to encase the entire Empire State Building in ice. One of the X-Men, Storm, followed up with a wave of intense heat, and a blast of electricity. Unable to stand the sudden temperature shifts, N'astirh exploded (*Uncanny X-Men* #242, March 1989). Pryor subsequently perished in combat against her double, Jean Grey (*X-Factor* #38, March 1989). With the demons' magic defeated, the Empire State Building reverted to normalcy.

System Crash was a team of criminal computer hackers who worked for the subversive organization Hydra. One of System Crash's members, Wirehead, hacked into the controls for the Empire State Building's security systems, enabling Hydra soldiers to take over the entire building. Daredevil, Silver Sable, and her mercenary team, the Wild Pack, managed to infiltrate the building to take on the villains. The Wild Pack battled Hydra, and Daredevil fought Wirehead, who finally escaped (*Daredevil*, vol. 1, #328, May 1994).

In Norse mythology Garm is the enormous wolf that guards the entrance to the underworld ruled by the death goddess, Hela. On his mistress's orders, Garm took mental possession of the armor of the invincible Destroyer and attacked the thunder god, Thor, in New York. Subsequently, Thor and his ally Thunderstrike went to the Empire State Building to survey the city and find the Destroyer (*Thor*, vol. 1, #477, August 1994).

Peter Parker accompanied his aunt May to the Empire State Building, where she informed him that she knew he was Spider-Man. Shortly afterward, she died (*Amazing Spider-Man*, vol. 1, #400, April 1995). It turned out that this "Aunt May" was actu-

EMPIRE STATE BUILDING

ally an impostor, but the real Aunt May eventually learned of her nephew Peter's dual identity as well.

Posing as human, a member of the alien, shape-shifting race of Skrulls infiltrated Hydra and became its leader. Calling himself the Sensational Hydra, he captured Captain America on the Empire State Building's observation deck (*Captain America*, vol. 3, #5, May 1998).

A cyborg known simply as the Russian battled Spider-Man and the Punisher atop the Empire State Building and fell off. He plummeted through the sidewalk to the underground, only to be hit by a subway train. But this cyborg was far tougher than the Armadillo, and he survived! (*The Punisher*, vol. 5, #2, August 2001.)

In the final shot of the first *Spider-Man* movie (2002), the web-slinger perches triumphantly atop the spire of the Empire State Building, overlooking the city.

In the alternate continuity of Marvel's Ultimate line of comics, the investment firm Fenris International, headed by the unscrupulous Andrea and Andreas von Strucker, is based in the Empire State Building, where they are clearly up to no good (*Ultimate X-Men* #51, November 2004).

After all this hectic activity, things have lately been quiet at the Empire State Building, but that's not likely to last for long. *

MARVEL COMICS

MARVEL PUBLISHING, THE DIVISION of Marvel Entertainment that creates the comics, is located in New York, as the Marvel Comics offices have always been.

Marvel was originally known as Timely Publications, when publisher Martin Goodman founded his comics line in 1939. Timely was initially based at Goodman's offices in the McGraw-Hill Building at 330 West Forty-second Street. With Timely's growing success, the company moved to an impressive address, Suite 1401 of the Empire State Building.

In the 1960s and early 1970s, Stan Lee and his Marvel Bull-pen were based at 635 Madison Avenue, though it was Marvel's parent company's address, 625, that was printed in the comics. Later in the 1970s, Marvel moved down the street to 575 Madison Avenue, then moved downtown in the 1980s to 387 Park Avenue South.

In the 1990s, Marvel relocated to 10 East Fortieth Street, just off Fifth Avenue, near the New York Public Library's Humanities and Social Sciences Library at Fifth and Forty-second Street. In the first *Spider-Man* movie (2002), Peter Parker's beloved uncle Ben is killed across Fifth Avenue from the library.

The Marvel editorial offices are currently located nearby, at 417 Fifth Avenue.

Every once in a while Marvel writers and artists engage in metafictional playfulness and set part of a story in the company's own offices. In *Amazing Fantasy* #12 (May 1962) a little man came to the Marvel offices to sell his story, but writer/editor Stan Lee and artist Steve Ditko showed him the door; they didn't realize the little man was actually from the Fifth Dimension. Doctor Doom once showed up at the Marvel

offices to confront his own creators, Stan Lee and Jack Kirby (*Fantastic Four*, vol. 1, #10, January 1963). If you want to see what Stan Lee looked like before he grew his trademark mustache, take a look at him saying hello as Daredevil swings by the Marvel offices' window (*Daredevil*, vol. 1, #29, June 1967). That prankster from outer space, the Impossible Man, threw the Marvel offices into chaos in *Fantastic Four*, vol. 1, #176 (November 1976), then made a return visit in *Uncanny X-Men Annual* #7 (1983). Stan met the teenage Super Hero Nova, but turned down his bid to star in his own comic book in *Nova*, vol. 1, #5 (January 1977). Stan suffered no repercussions from that, but the She-Hulk knocked her writer/artist John Byrne out the office window in *Sensational She-Hulk* #50 (April 1993)! ✺

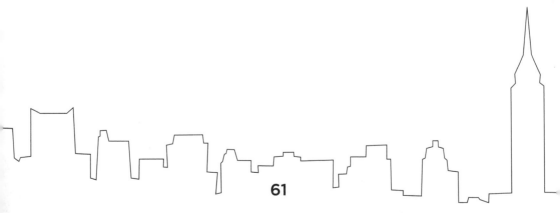

TUDOR CITY
Fortieth Street to Forty-third Street between First and Second Avenues

IN 1925 REAL ESTATE mogul Fred F. French began construction on Tudor City, a cluster of a dozen apartment buildings on the East Side of midtown Manhattan. The development took its name from the Tudor architectural style, which was a major influence on architect H. Douglas Ives in designing the buildings. Built upon high ground, Tudor City offers a measure of isolation from the bustling streets of midtown. Tudor City was completed in 1928 and designated a historic district in 1988. It remains a desirable address for upscale city living.

In the first *Spider-Man* movie, industrialist Norman Osborn, who eventually becomes the criminal Green Goblin, lives in a palatial apartment in Tudor City. Norman's son, Harry, has taken over the apartment in *Spider-Man 2*. Here, Doctor Octopus delivers the captured Spider-Man to Harry, who unmasks him. It is also here that Harry discovers secret rooms that contain the Green Goblin's equipment.

However, the interior of Osborn's apartment was actually shot at the Greystone Mansion, at 905 Loma Vista Drive in Beverly Hills, California. Constructed from 1926 to 1928, it was the home of millionaire Edward L. Doheny Jr., who died only four months after moving in, and his family. Comprising sixty-seven rooms, Greystone is the largest family residence in Beverly Hills. ✳

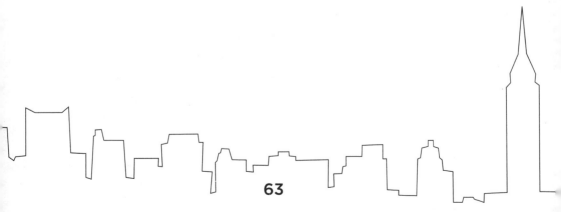

UNITED NATIONS
760 United Nations Plaza

THE UNITED NATIONS IS an international organization to which the vast majority of the world's countries belong. In the aftermath of World War II, fifty nations signed the United Nations Charter on June 26, 1945. Once the nations had ratified the charter, the United Nations was officially born on October 24 of that year. Since then, the membership has expanded to include 192 nations, all of which are represented in the UN's General Assembly.

The United Nations headquarters was constructed in 1949 and 1950 on a sixteen-acre site in Manhattan along the East River and officially opened on January 9, 1951. The headquarters site is legally considered to be international territory, and not part of the United States.

UNITED NATIONS

The UN mediates disputes between different nations and enforces international law. Among the UN's other stated goals are the promotion of human rights and the prevention of war.

In the Marvel Universe the United Nations performs various other significant functions as well.

The United Nations and its Security Council both "recognized and fully sanctioned" the Super Hero team the Avengers as a "peacekeeping force" in the team's original charter. Although the Maria Stark Foundation was the Avengers' principal source of financial support, the United Nations agreed to provide the team with additional funding.

The international law enforcement, counterterrorism, and intelligence organization SHIELD is an arm of the United Nations, although sometimes Marvel has depicted SHIELD as a wholly American operation.

The United Nations oversees the Savage Land, a tropical jungle on the Antarctic continent, which is inhabited by prehistoric animals including dinosaurs, and which was created by extraterrestrial technology. The UN treats the Savage Land as a wildlife preserve and forbids its commercial exploitation.

The UN also financed and launched Starcore, an international space station that is dedicated to studying the sun.

The United Nations has recognized as sovereign nations Genosha, an island nation formerly populated by mutants;

Latveria, the monarchy ruled by Doctor Doom; Lemuria, the home of the Deviants race, an evolutionary offshoot of humanity; Symkaria, the pocket kingdom whose best-known citizen is the mercenary Silver Sable; and Wakanda, the monarchy ruled by the Black Panther. All are members of the United Nations.

The United Nations headquarters' real and symbolic importance as a forum for the nations of the world has made it a continual target for would-be conquerors, terrorists, fanatics, criminals, and alien invaders in the Marvel Universe. The building might as well have a giant bull's-eye painted on top.

In the 1950s, Soviet agent Albert Malik usurped the identity of the Red Skull, a Nazi war criminal. This new Red Skull broke into the newly opened United Nations building and took the delegates hostage. There he was confronted by the Captain America of the 1950s (replacing the original), who was making his first public appearance (*Young Men* #24, December 1953).

During his rampage through New York City, the gargantuan alien infant Monsteroso ended up climbing atop the United Nations building, as if he were a misplaced King Kong. He was shot with a harpoon filled with sedatives and tumbled into the East River (*Adventures* #5, October 1961).

An arrogant unnamed alien who considered himself to be a champion in all sports arrived at the United Nations building, where he set the human race a challenge. Unless they could best him in physical or mental competition, his race would invade Earth. No one could match the champion's various superpowers. But then a wily reporter, Frank Taylor, conned the foolish alien into a sleeping contest. Taylor claimed that a human could sleep for a million years, whereupon the champion put himself into suspended animation for 2 million years (*Strange Tales*, vol. 1, #98, July 1962). If only every alien invasion could be dealt with so easily!

Prince Namor the Sub-Mariner, monarch of the undersea kingdom of Atlantis, demanded that the Fantastic Four inform the United Nations that Atlantis would forbid the people of the surface world to travel on the oceans or in the skies. Soon afterward Fantastic Four leader Reed Richards addressed a session of the General Assembly to convey Namor's ultimatum. A man calling himself Dr. G. W. Falton then recounted the origin of the Atlanteans and the Sub-Mariner to the General Assembly. After concluding his speech, "Falton" threw off his disguise, revealed himself as Prince Namor, and declared war on the human race. Subsequently, Atlantean forces invaded Earth's leading cities, only to be defeated when Reed Richards created a device that evaporated the water in the invading, Atlanteans' helmets. (*Fantastic Four Annual* #1, 1963).

In subsequent years Namor's enmity toward the surface

world has abated, and he has repeatedly attempted to persuade the United Nations to grant membership to Atlantis.

Candy Southern, the girlfriend of Warren Worthington, the X-Men's Angel, had her first job working at the United Nations (*X-Men*, vol. 1, #31, April 1967).

In the first of his many encounters with the United Nations, the mutant terrorist Magneto, accompanied by Quicksilver and the Scarlet Witch, invaded the General Assembly to demand that the human race surrender to mutantkind. A small number of Avengers tried but failed to capture Magneto, who was nonetheless forced to retreat (*Avengers*, vol. 1, #49, February 1968).

A costumed fanatic called the Super-Patriot so hated foreigners being on American soil that he attempted to obliterate the United Nations building with his Ultimate Weapon. SHIELD agents smashed the weapon, and the Super-Patriot fell to his death (*Nick Fury, Agent of SHIELD*, vol. 1, #13, July 1969).

Saburo Yoshida, Japan's ambassador to the United Nations, was the father of Shiro, the Super Hero known as Sunfire. Saburo was killed by his terrorist brother Tomo, who was in turn slain by the vengeful Sunfire (*X-Men*, vol. 1, #64, January 1970).

The Asian mastermind known as the Yellow Claw attempted to destroy the United Nations building from his flying warship, the *Sky Dragon*, but was stopped by SHIELD director Nick

Fury (*Strange Tales*, vol. 3, #1, November 1994, but set much earlier).

Magneto, using ancient texts he uncovered in Carlsbad Caverns, genetically engineered Alpha the Ultimate Mutant, a being of incalculable power. Alpha teleported Magneto and his Brotherhood of Evil Mutants to the United Nations building, where Magneto demanded (again) that the nations of the world surrender to him. On Magneto's command, Alpha levitated the entire United Nations building into the air, as a demonstration of power. Magneto's longtime antagonist, Professor Charles Xavier, and the sorcerer Doctor Strange persuaded Alpha to turn against Magneto. Alpha then devolved Magneto and the Brotherhood into infants and departed into outer space (*Defenders* #16, October 1974).

Doctor Doom dispatched some of his robot guards to the United Nations to present the organization with a statue of himself, seemingly as a gift. Inside the statue Doom had secreted a device through which he could control the minds of the UN representatives, but the Fantastic Four foiled his scheme (*Fantastic Four* #200, November 1978).

For whatever reason, the menaces of the Marvel Universe left the UN pretty much alone in the 1980s, but made up for lost time in the following decade.

According to the 1990 graphic novel *Silver Surfer: The*

UNITED NATIONS

Enslavers, an alien race by that name not only conquered Earth, but also imprisoned the planet's entire population in immense holding chambers. The Enslavers' overlord, Mrrungo-Mu, briefly made the United Nations complex his headquarters. The Silver Surfer ultimately bested Mrrungo-Mu in combat, freeing Earth. (It is likely that this story depicts an alternate timeline since normal Marvel continuity never refers to the Enslavers' conquest of Earth.)

Doctor Demonicus, a genetic engineer who has used his expertise to create monsters, took control of a Pacific island he called Demonica and sought recognition as a sovereign nation from the United Nations (*Avengers West Coast* #74, September 1991; #93–94, April–May 1993).

Around the same time, Baron Wolfgang Von Strucker, the head of the subversive organization Hydra, masterminded an attack on the United Nations complex, but was thwarted by his perennial nemesis, SHIELD director Nick Fury (*Nick Fury, Agent of SHIELD,* vol. 2, #47, May 1993).

The superhuman being Adam Warlock appeared at the United Nations to demand that his base, Monster Island, be recognized as a sovereign nation. Warlock was attacked at the UN by the satanic Man-Beast and his ally, the superevolved warthog called Triax the Terrible, but defeated them both (*Warlock and the Infinity Watch* #28, May 1994).

With the Hulk under their control, the superpowered team of mercenaries called the U-Foes once attacked the United Nations. The new Heroes for Hire team freed the Hulk and forced the U-Foes to flee (*Heroes for Hire* #1, July 1997).

The Egyptian death god Seth, working through mortal agents, sought to destroy the United Nations building as part of his plot to plunge Earth into nuclear war. The Super Hero Moon Knight foiled Seth by destroying a statue in his image, which was the repository of his magic (*Moon Knight,* vol. 4, #4, April 1998).

The Masters of Evil, a vast organization of Super Villains, held the United Nations building for a ransom of $1 trillion. A new team of Super Heroes, the Thunderbolts, saved the day by capturing most of the Masters (*Thunderbolts*, vol. 1, #25, April 1999).

About that same time, Magneto unleashed an electromagnetic pulse that deactivated electrical devices all over the world. In appeasement, the United Nations awarded Magneto sovereignty over the island nation of Genosha, which had a large population of mutants (*X-Men*, vol. 2, #87, April 1999). Of course, this stratagem did not work. One of Magneto's Acolytes, Johanna Cargill, became Genosha's ambassador to the United Nations. Eventually she delivered an ultimatum at the UN demanding that the world surrender to Magneto and

Genosha (*X-Men*, vol. 2, #111, April 2001), but the X-Men ultimately thwarted the Genoshan attempt at conquest.

The Scarlet Centurion appeared on the United Nations Plaza to herald the imminent arrival of his father, Kang the Conqueror, the warlord from the far future. The Avengers battled the Centurion there, until Kang himself arrived and demolished a nearby building (*Avengers*, vol. 3, #41, June 2001).

Perhaps in response to the "Magneto War," the United Nations briefly employed a short-lived spin-off team from the X-Men, the X-Treme Sanctions Executive, led by Storm, as a global superhuman police force (*X-Treme X-Men* #1, July 2001).

In an alternate timeline, Thor, as monarch of Asgard, conquered Earth and appeared at the United Nations to address his new subjects (*Thor*, Vol. 2, #55, January 2003).

Sooner or later, one of the many attempts to demolish the UN building inevitably succeeded. This was no terrorist assault, but another round in the Great Game, whereby high rollers gambled on the outcome of battles they staged between superpowered opponents. As part of the "game," the costumed criminals Joystick, Polestar, and Tremolo contended against Mr. Fantastic, Sub-Mariner, and the Thunderbolts at the United Nations. The gaming council activated bombs that had been planted in the building. The Super Heroes prevented the building from collapsing, but there was still considerable debris (*New Thunderbolts* #3, February 2005).

Still, the damage could not have been that extensive, because shortly thereafter the mutant Apocalypse turned up at the UN. There he demanded that they slaughter 90 percent of their nations' populations, or he would do it for them by releasing a lethal plague (*X-Men*, Vol. 2, #185, June 2006). Luckily, neither disaster took place.

But soon afterward, the United Nations building was blown up yet again, this time inadvertently. The accidental culprit was Speed, a member of the Young Avengers. The criminal organization Zodiac took control of the remains of the UN complex, but the Young Avengers overcame them (*Young Avengers* #12, August 2006). The UN complex was quickly rebuilt. ✳

GEM THEATER
Forty-second Street between Broadway and Eighth Avenue

AS THE CLASSIC 1933 movie musical of the same name suggests, Forty-second Street was once the heart of Broadway, a place of theatrical magic, excitement, and glamour. But as the twentieth century wore on, Forty-second Street, between Broadway and Eighth Avenue, degenerated into one of the tawdriest areas of the city. The theaters fell into disrepair or were turned into porn-movie houses. Drug dealers and thieves prowled the street. Shootings were not uncommon. Most tourists knew better than to venture the few blocks down from the rest of the theater district onto Forty-second Street.

Using this milieu as a backdrop, Marvel responded to the popular "blaxploitation" films of the 1970s with the series *Luke Cage, Hero for Hire*. Cage, later known as Power Man, was one of the first African-American Super Heroes. But he wasn't wealthy like Tony Stark (Iron Man), so Cage offered his crime-fighting services in exchange for money.

Cage set up his "Hero for Hire" office above the Gem Theater, a run-down movie house on Forty-second Street. The Gem was managed by Cage's friend D. W. Griffith, a film buff, who took pleasure in sharing the same name as the famous film director of the silent-movie era.

Visitors to the Gem should be warned to avoid its infamous "soda machine from hell." As Cage can attest, the machine seems to be alive, intelligent, and malevolent, continually finding new ways to thwart his efforts to get a drink out of it.

In the 1990s, Forty-second Street underwent a radical rehabilitation, spearheaded by the Walt Disney Company's restoration and reopening of the New Amsterdam Theater, the former home of the legendary Ziegfeld Follies.

Today the "new Forty-second Street" is one of New York's leading centers of tourist activities, with restored theaters for plays and movies, the New York branch of Madame Tussauds Wax Museum, and skyscrapers housing the headquarters of corporate giants.

If the Gem Theater is still there, it has probably been bought and remodeled by a major theater chain. It is unlikely that D.W., or even Cage himself, could afford the rents on Forty-second Street nowadays. ✳

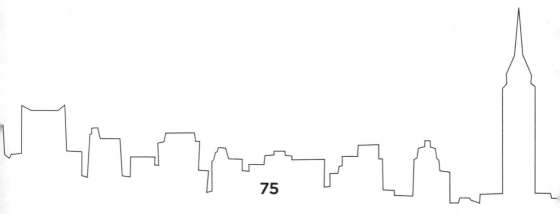

MADISON SQUARE GARDEN
Seventh Avenue between Thirty-first and Thirty-third Streets

KNOWN AS THE WORLD'S Most Famous Arena, Madison Square Garden is New York City's foremost venue for sports events, popular-music concerts, and political conventions. The immense hall can seat over thirty-nine thousand spectators for concerts, but less than twenty thousand for sporting events.

But oddly, Madison Square Garden, which sits atop Pennsylvania Station on Manhattan's West Side, is nowhere near Madison Square, which is located on the East Side between Twenty-third and Twenty-sixth streets.

It was across from this park, on Madison Avenue and Twenty-sixth Street, that the original Madison Square Garden once stood. The building originally served as a railroad depot until the opening of Grand Central Depot (the predecessor of Grand Central Terminal) in 1871. Circus impresario P. T. Barnum bought the building and converted it into an arena called Barnum's Monster Classical and Geological Hippodrome. In 1876 it was renamed Gilmore's Garden, after a bandleader of the time, and in 1879 its new owner, William Henry Vanderbilt, reopened the arena as Madison Square Garden.

In 1890 the second Madison Square Garden opened at the same location. The second-tallest building in the city at that time, the new Garden was designed by the celebrated architect Stanford White. Ironically, White was murdered in the Garden's rooftop restaurant in 1906 (as depicted in the novel *Ragtime*). This Madison Square Garden off Madison Square no longer exists, although the statue of the goddess Diana that once stood atop the building survives today in the Philadelphia Museum of Art.

Boxing promoter Tex Rickard built a new arena, which opened in 1925, and even though it was located at Fiftieth Street and Eighth Avenue, he named it Madison Square Garden after its celebrated predecessors. This building likewise no longer exists.

Finally, following the controversial demolition of the original Pennsylvania Station, the current Madison Square Garden opened in 1968 in its place. The current Penn Station is underground, beneath the Garden, and the Garden, together with the surrounding office buildings, make up a complex known as Pennsylvania (or Penn) Plaza.

Madison Square Garden is the home of the city's NBA team, the New York Knicks; its WNBA team, the New York Liberty; and its hockey team, the New York Rangers. The Garden has been a famous venue for boxing matches and was formerly a site for World Wrestling Entertainment events.

The Democratic National Convention was held at Madison Square Garden in 1976, 1980, and 1992, and the Republican National Convention was held there in 2004.

Madison Square Garden has long been a famous venue for rock concerts. Among the major performers who have appeared there are John Lennon, Elvis Presley, Frank Sinatra, the Rolling Stones, Bruce Springsteen, U2, the Grateful Dead, Billy Joel, and, more frequently than anyone else, Elton John.

Ringling Brothers and Barnum Bailey circus performs regularly at the Garden. The Garden's Expo Center has even housed comic book conventions.

And why not? Marvel has set a number of stories at the Garden over the last six decades.

Back in the 1940s the Reaper, a demagogue who claimed to be a visionary prophet, held a rally at Madison Square Garden. (*Captain America Comics* #22, January 1943). In actuality the Reaper was a Nazi agent, who subsequently perished while fleeing Captain America.

In *Amazing Spider-Man* #16 (September 1964), the Ringmaster and his Circus of Crime gave a performance at the largest venue in Manhattan, which presumably was Madison Square

Garden. Using his hypnotic hat, the Ringmaster mesmerized the audience, but Daredevil and Spider-Man foiled his attempt to rob them all. This would prove to be only the first of Daredevil and Spider-Man's many appearances at the Garden.

The mysterious criminal mastermind known as the Masked Marauder created an android he called the Tri-Man, since it possessed the mental and physical abilities of three men. To impress members of the Maggia, a criminal syndicate, the Marauder dispatched his Tri-Man to Madison Square Garden for a public battle with Daredevil. Fighting within an actual boxing ring, Daredevil, the son of a boxer, bested the android (*Daredevil*, vol. 1, #22, November 1966). Daredevil would later have a fight with Captain America at the Garden as well (*Daredevil*, vol. 1, #43, August 1968).

When the criminal organization Zodiac captured Manhattan Island and held it for ransom, its mercenary army herded the citizenry into Madison Square Garden (*Avengers,* vol. 1, #82, November 1970). Having captured members of the Avengers, Zodiac's masked leader, Aries, planned to execute them at the Garden on live television. Daredevil rescued the Avengers, and together they defeated Zodiac and freed the people of Manhattan.

Stunt cyclist Johnny Blaze sold his soul to the demon Mephisto to prevent his stepfather, "Crash" Simpson, from dying of a rare blood disease. But the cunning Mephisto had not promised to prevent Simpson's death by other means. When the Simpson Cycle Show appeared at Madison Square Garden, Simpson died in a motorcycle crash. Subsequently, Mephisto transformed Blaze into the Ghost Rider, a demonic motorcyclist with a flaming skull (*Marvel Spotlight* #5, August 1972).

Subsequently, Blaze headed the performance of "Ghost Rider's Motorcycle Extravaganza" at Madison Square Garden. But the show was interrupted by the Orb, a motorcycle-gang leader who took Blaze's girlfriend, Roxanne Simpson, hostage. Present in the audience as Peter Parker, Spider-Man joined forces with Ghost Rider to rescue Roxanne and defeat the Orb, who became Blaze's archenemy (*Marvel Team-Up* #15, November 1973).

Alejandro Cortez, a murderous scientist who invented a device that could endow him with the abilities of animals, joined a circus that was performing at Madison Square Garden. There, under the name Lionfang, he battled "hero for hire" Luke Cage (*Luke Cage, Hero for Hire* #13, September 1973). Damek the Earth-Shaker, an ally of the Super Hero Darkhawk, also once worked as a performer at the Garden (*Darkhawk* #50, April 1995).

The costumed assassin Bullseye once lured his enemy Daredevil over to Madison Square Garden, where a circus was performing. The ensuing battle between Daredevil and Bullseye was broadcast on live television (*Daredevil,* vol. 1, #131, March 1976).

The humanoid wolf called the Man-Beast, working through human pawns, organized a phony religious cult, the Legion of the Light, which held a rally at Madison Square Garden. The Man-Beast plotted to massacre the attendees, but was thwarted by Spider-Man and the Southern Super Hero Razorback (*Spectacular Spider-Man* #15, February 1978).

Captain America returned to the Garden to put on a motor-cycle stunt show with Team America, later known as the Thunderiders (*Captain America,* vol. 1, #269, May 1982).

The team of Power Man and Iron Fist, known as Heroes for Hire Inc., prevented the terrorist Black Tigers from blowing up Madison Square Garden (*Power Man and Iron Fist* #105, May 1984). Years later another terrorist attack was made at the Garden by the Elements of Doom, artificial creatures that are each composed of a different chemical element (*Thunderbolts,* vol. 1, #6, September 1997).

Since Madison Square Garden has served as the locale for the Democratic and Republican national conventions, it may well have also been the setting for the All-Night Party convention that nominated Howard the Duck for president. Howard accepted, but lost the election when he was photographed taking a bubble bath with campaign worker Beverly Switzler (*Howard the Duck,* vol. 1, #7, December 1976).

Another presidential candidate who appeared at Madison Square Garden was Randall Shire, a mutant who could enslave people with the sound of his voice. The mutant warrior Cable thwarted an attempt to assassinate Shire at the Garden, but also discredited him as a candidate (*Cable* #82, August 2000).

In an alternate reality, the Martians from H. G. Wells's *War of the Worlds* conquered Earth in 2001. The leader of Earth's resistance to the Martian conquerors is Killraven, who had been trained as a gladiator for the Martians' amusement. The Martians staged gladiatorial contests at Madison Square Garden, which they renamed the Arena. Once, Killraven was captured and made to face off in the Arena against the Slasher, a seemingly genetically engineered giant with a robotic arm. Luckily, Killraven quickly defeated his larger opponent (*Amazing Adventures,* vol. 2, #19, July 1973). ✳

ROCKEFELLER CENTER

Forty-eighth to Fifty-first Streets, between Fifth Avenue and Avenue of the Americas

ORIGINALLY DEVELOPED BY John D. Rockefeller Jr., Rockefeller Center is the world's largest commercial building complex. Spreading over twenty-two acres in midtown Manhattan, the Center includes nineteen buildings. The original fourteen buildings constructed in the 1930s, are monumental examples of the art deco style of that period.

The most prominent building in the Center is the GE Building, formerly known as the RCA Building, which towers seventy floors over Rockefeller Plaza. At present it is the seventh-tallest building in the city. (Two taller buildings are currently under construction.)

The headquarters of the NBC television network is in the GE Building, including studios for programs such as *Late Night with Conan O'Brien. Saturday Night Live* has been telecast from the building's Studio 8H for over thirty years. The NBC sitcom *30 Rock* is named after the GE Building's address, 30 Rockefeller Plaza. The *Today* show is telecast from the ground-level Studio 1A, across the street from the GE Building.

The Rainbow Room, a celebrated restaurant and nightspot, is on the sixty-fifth floor of the GE Building, affording spectacular views of the Center. The top of the GE Building is known

ROCKEFELLER CENTER

as the Top of the Rock and offers its own breathtaking views of the city.

In front of the GE Building is a sunken plaza with a fountain featuring Paul Manship's enormous sculpture of Prometheus, the Titan of Greek mythology who gave humanity the gift of fire. In the Marvel Universe, Prometheus, like the other gods of classical mythology, is real: he first appeared in a Marvel Super Hero title in *Avengers,* vol. 1, #282 (August 1987).

Elsewhere in Rockefeller Center, on Fifth Avenue facing St. Patrick's Cathedral, is an art deco statue of Prometheus' brother, Atlas, carrying an immense sphere representing the heavens, by Lee Lawrie and Rene Chambellan. Atlas is real in the Marvel Universe, too: he first appeared in *Journey into Mystery,* vol. 1, #124 (January 1966).

However, perhaps the most famous building in Rockefeller Center is Radio City Music Hall, known as the Showplace of the Nation. Another masterpiece of art deco design, the Music Hall is the world's largest indoor theater, holding 5,933 seats. The Music Hall opened in 1932 and from 1933 to 1979 typically presented a feature film along with a stage show, famously featuring the precision dancers called the Rockettes. Today the Music Hall is primarily a venue for concerts and awards shows such as Broadway's Tony Awards. In 2006, Stephen King, the writer of *The Dark Tower* series of novels, on which Marvel based a comics series in 2007, gave a benefit performance at the Music Hall along with fellow authors J. K. Rowling and John Irving.

The offices of Simon & Schuster, the publishers of this book, are located in another Rockefeller Center building, at 1230 Avenue of the Americas.

Rockefeller Center is the New York City location that is most associated with Christmas. Every year an enormous Christmas tree, from seventy-five to ninety feet tall, is erected in front of the GE Building; the lighting of the tree is telecast nationwide. Each winter the sunken plaza is transformed into an ice-skating rink, and Radio City Music Hall hosts its traditional Christmas show.

After rescuing Mary Jane Watson in the first *Spider-Man* movie (2002), the web-slinger leaves her in the rooftop garden atop 620 Fifth Avenue, in the Rockefeller Center complex.

Rufus T. Hackstabber is a taxi driver who bears a remarkable resemblance to a certain 1930s movie comedian with glasses, a mustache, and an omnipresent cigar. Robbed of a $7.80 cab fare by thieves, the fast-talking Hackstabber persuaded Shang-Chi, Master of Kung Fu, to help him hunt them down. The persistent Hackstabber ended up confronting the thieves' boss, the criminal mastermind Tiger-Claw, at Rockefeller Center. Shang-Chi not only defeated Tiger-Claw, but rewarded Hackstabber with $7.80 (*Giant-Size Master of Kung Fu* #4, June 1975).

On the first Christmas since the formation of the "new" X-Men, the team members gathered at Rockefeller Center, overlooking the skating rink. Other familiar faces were also present, including Nick Fury, Matt Murdock, X-Men writer Chris Claremont, X-Men artist Dave Cockrum, X-Men creators Stan Lee and Jack Kirby, and legendary DC Comics editor Julius Schwartz. Scott Summers and Jean Grey (alias Cyclops and Marvel Girl) left for a romantic dinner at a Rockefeller Center restaurant over sixty flights up: this makes it the celebrated Rainbow Room, on the sixty-fifth floor of the GE Building. Unfortunately, the X-Men's holiday bliss was ruined when the Sentinels, mutant-hunting robots, attacked (*Uncanny X-Men* #98, April 1976).

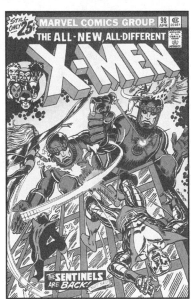

The members of the Gotham Game Club, all of whom were war veterans, decided to compete at destroying the Hulk when he next appeared in New

York City. Club member Franklin Knight drove a car outfitted with laser guns in an attack on the Hulk at Rockefeller Center, but the Hulk flung the car into a building, wrecking the vehicle and trapping Knight inside it (*Incredible Hulk Annual* #9, 1980).

A hit man called Ice tracked Moon Knight at Rockefeller Center, shot at him with his rifle, and saw the costumed crimefighter fall behind the skating rink. But when Ice went to inspect the body, Moon Knight attacked him, and Ice only narrowly escaped (*Moon Knight*, vol. 1, #4, February 1981).

One year on Christmas Eve the X-Men's computer Cerebro detected the presence of an immensely powerful mutant at Rockefeller Center. Several X-Men headed to the complex to investigate. There they battled members of the Brotherhood of Evil Mutants, who were also looking for this mysterious mutant. Then a man appeared who called himself Kris Kringle and wore a Santa Claus costume. He seemingly turned the Brotherhood members into toys, then teleported the X-Men several blocks away. No longer able to remember their encounter with the mysterious Mr. Kringle, the X-Men celebrated Christmas with other teammates at Rockefeller Center (*Marvel Holiday Special* #1, 1991).

A criminal named Elias Flynn used his mind-control powers to force a group of superpowered young people called the

Metahumes to rob a bank in Rockefeller Center (*Spider-Man: Friends and Enemies* #2, February 1995).

Years later, another group of X-Men gathered socially at Rockefeller Center shortly before Christmas, but without any unusual incident (*Uncanny X-Men* #341, February 1997).

The most noteworthy Marvel stories set at Rockefeller Center take place in the NBC television studios in the former RCA Building.

When Peter Parker decided that he would be "Spider-Man no more!" he discarded his costume in a trash can. The costume found its way into the hands of Spider-Man's longtime nemesis *Daily Bugle* publisher J. Jonah Jameson, who was ecstatic that the web-slinger had retired. Soon Jameson was a guest on *The Tonight Show Starring Johnny Carson,* which was based in New York City in the 1960s. Announcer Ed McMahon displayed the costume to the cameras, but Johnny Carson clearly regarded the pompous Jameson with wry irony (*Amazing Spider-Man* #50, July 1967).

Later, Spider-Man battled the Silver Samurai during a telecast of *Saturday Night Live,* hosted by none other than Stan Lee, with the Hulk's friend Rick Jones, a rock musician, as the musical guest. This story featured *SNL*'s original "Not Ready for Prime Time Players" Dan Aykroyd, John Belushi, Jane Curtin, Garrett Morris, Bill Murray, Laraine Newman, and Gilda Radner and climaxed with a duel between the Silver Samurai and Belushi's own samurai character (*Marvel Team-Up* #74, October 1978).

A decade later, Wonder Man persuaded several of his fellow Avengers to accompany him on his appearance on *Late Night with David Letterman*. Mad-scientist wannabe Fabian Stankowitz interrupted the show to attack the Avengers, but Letterman himself knocked out Stankowitz with an oversize doorknob (*Avengers,* vol. 1, #239, January 1984).

Since then no Marvel character has appeared on an NBC show based in Rockefeller Center in the comics, although in 2002 *Tonight Show* host Jay Leno met Spider-Man in a serial that ran as a backup feature in various Marvel titles. ✳

TIMES SQUARE
From West Fortieth to West Fifty-third Streets, between Sixth and Eighth Avenues

OFTEN CONSIDERED THE heart of New York City, Times Square is most famous around the world as the place where hundreds of thousands of enthusiastic people gather each December 31 to celebrate the coming of the New Year. Even Marvel's sorcerer supreme, Doctor Strange, once took his beloved Clea, a princess from another dimension, to Times Square one New Year's Eve. There Strange encountered an old friend: novelist Tom Wolfe, the first important mainstream writer to mention Marvel Comics in one of his books (*Doctor Strange,* vol. 1, #180, May 1969).

The New Year's Eve crowds come to watch a large Waterford crystal ball being lowered from atop the building at One Times Square at the stroke of midnight. One Times Square was once the headquarters of one of the world's great newspapers, *The New York Times*, and it is for this newspaper that Times Square received its name in 1904. The *Times* moved to another building a few blocks up Broadway in 1913, and the newspaper company has recently constructed a new headquarters on Eighth Avenue across from the Port Authority Bus Terminal, but the Times Square moniker remains.

On New Year's Eve and other special occasions, the streets in the Times Square area are closed to traffic so that crowds of pedestrians can gather there. For example, in the first *Spider-Man* movie (2002), New Yorkers gather in Times Square to hear Macy Gray play at the "World Unity Festival." When the Green Goblin attacks the festival, Spider-Man appears and battles him. Much of this sequence was actually filmed in a mock-up of Times Square built in California.

Spider-Man 3 (2007) features a vignette in the real Times Square in which Spider-Man's co-creator Stan Lee encounters actor Tobey Maguire as Peter Parker.

Times Square is, of course, also famous for its enormous billboards, video screens, and electronic and neon signs.

The Captain America and Bucky of the 1950s were appearing at a festival in Times Square celebrating American business when a large sign atop a building lit up with the message "Captain America Dies Today." The culprit was a superpowered

Soviet agent named Electro, who could absorb and discharge electricity (and who is not to be confused with Spider-Man's later costumed foe). Cap and Bucky battled and bested Electro inside the building, then returned to the festival. The sign was altered to read "Captain America Lives" (*Captain America Comics* #78, September 1954).

There was even a Super Villain named Typeface, who used to work for a sign company, who blew up many of the huge signs in Times Square until Spider-Man finally stopped him (*Peter Parker, Spider-Man,* vol. 2, #23, November 2000). Ironically, Typeface was later killed in Times Square in combat with Venom (*Civil War: Front Line* #10, December 2006). Venom also once fought Scream, a similar menace in a sentient alien costume, in Times Square (*Web of Spider-Man* #119, December 1994).

The famous street Broadway runs down Times Square, which is also the center of New York's Broadway theater district, the most famous in the world. In *Spider-Man 3,* Mary Jane Watson has a lead role in a Broadway musical playing at the Broadhurst Theatre at 235 West Forty-fourth Street.

Considering Times Square's central location and wide streets, it is not surprising that it has been an arena for many battles between Super Heroes and Super Villains.

In his first appearance as a Super Villain, the Molecule Man raised the Baxter Building, the Fantastic Four's headquarters, and caused it to hover ominously over Times Square (*Fantastic Four*, vol. 1, #20, November 1963).

While temporarily endowed with "cosmic" powers, Spider-Man overpowered Hydro-Man, the Rhino, and the Shocker in a single fight in Times Square. Considering Spider-Man a menace as well, the ungrateful Times Square onlookers started throwing rocks at their savior (*Spectacular Spider-Man*, vol. 1, #160, January 1990).

The Zombie, formerly a man named Simon Garth, once wreaked havoc in Times Square and even captured Spider-Man when the web-slinger tried to stop him (*Spider-Man Unlimited*, vol. 1, #20, May 1998).

Doctor Octopus abducted the Palestinian foreign minister and held him hostage, risking the outbreak of war. He demanded that Spider-Man unmask in Times Square in exchange for the minister's release. But as Spider-Man confronted Doc Ock in Times Square, the minister was rescued, and Octopus fled in defeat (*Spectacular Spider-Man*, vol. 2, #8–10, February–April 2004).

Times Square was also the site of the climatic battle of the recent Civil War of Marvel's Super Heroes, ending when Captain America and his side surrendered to Iron Man (*Civil War* #7, 2007).

In the alternate continuity of Marvel's Ultimate line of comics, the X-Men's Beast helped rescue Iceman from the mutant-hunting Sentinel robots in Times Square; Wolverine clashed with his rival Sabretooth there; and the Sub-Mariner faced off there against the Invisible Woman. ✳

FOGWELL'S GYM AND JOSIE'S BAR & GRILL

From Thirty-fourth and Fifty-seventh Streets between Eighth Avenue and the
Hudson River

TODAY THE NEIGHBORHOOD OF Hell's Kitchen is often referred to as "Clinton," particularly by its residents, in no small part due to the fact that like many other formerly depressed areas of Manhattan, the neighborhood has undergone a considerable makeover in recent years. But this section of western Manhattan was once known as "the most dangerous area on the North American continent." According to legend, a young policeman, observing a riot taking place there, commented, "This place is hell itself," whereupon his older partner responded, "Hell's a mild climate. This is Hell's Kitchen."

Hell's Kitchen is the birthplace of two of Marvel's most important heroes: Matthew Murdock, the costumed crime fighter known as Daredevil, and Nick Fury, the World War II hero who became director of the international security agency SHIELD.

The neighborhood originated in the middle of the nineteenth century as Irish immigrants moved in, first into shantytowns and then into crowded tenements. (Murdock himself is Irish-American.) Widespread poverty spurred the rise of violent criminal gangs, one of which, the Gopher Gang, dominated the neighborhood at the turn of the century. Organized crime took over during Prohibition, and maintained its grip on Hell's Kitchen until the mid-1980s. From the 1950s on this Irish-American neighborhood has also seen an influx of Latino residents, particularly from Puerto Rico.

Criminal activity and gang feuds in Hell's Kitchen have inspired fictional tales ranging from the stories of Damon Runyon to the musical *West Side Story* to, of course, Marvel's *Daredevil* comics.

Over the last twenty years, however, Hell's Kitchen has radically changed. "Clinton" now attracts upper-middle-class residents and a community of actors and artists. Indeed, the real life Hell's Kitchen no longer bears much resemblance to the version seen in *Daredevil*, which was clearly inspired by the neighborhood's nefarious past.

Nick Fury grew up in Hell's Kitchen during the Great Depression, raised by his widowed mother along with his sister Dawn and brother Jake (*Strange Tales*, vol. 1, #159, August 1967, and *Sgt. Fury and His Howling Commandos* #68–69, July–August 1969). (Fury's aging process has been greatly slowed by the "Infinity Formula," a chemical concoction first administered to him at the end of World War II.) Jake grew up to become Nick's nemesis Scorpio, a founding member of the criminal organization Zodiac.

Matt Murdock was raised in Hell's Kitchen by his father, the small-time boxer "Battling Jack" Murdock. (Jack was estranged from his wife, Maggie, who became a nun, and Matt grew up incorrectly believing she was dead.) Jack used to train in the neighborhood at the fictional Fogwell's Gym. A local gangster, the Fixer, ordered Jack to throw his next fight, but Jack refused and won the match. The Fixer retaliated by having Jack murdered. Years later, Matt, in his costumed guise as Daredevil, confronted the Fixer and his thugs in Fogwell's Gym. Pursued by Daredevil into a nearby subway station, the terrified Fixer suffered a heart attack and died (*Daredevil*, vol. 1, 1964).

Years later, the Kingpin, New York's leading crime boss, temporarily ruined Matt Murdock's career as a lawyer and blew up his town house. A minor criminal stabbed Matt, who managed to get to Fogwell's Gym, where he collapsed. There he was found by his mother, Sister Maggie, who got him medical care (*Daredevil*, vol. 1, #229, April 1986).

Since then, Daredevil has considered himself the protector of Hell's Kitchen, and the neighborhood has continued to play an important part in the comic book series. Perhaps the most important of Daredevil's battles in Hell's Kitchen occured when the Kingpin sent the mentally unstable government agent Nuke to assassinate the crime fighter. The insane Nuke massacred innocent citizens in Hell's Kitchen until Daredevil finally succeeded in stopping him (*Daredevil*, vol. 1, #233, August 1986).

After "Battling Jack" Murdock's days, Fogwell's Gym fell into decline and disrepair, but in recent years Matt Murdock, again a successful lawyer, bought and restored the gymnasium that has proved to be a central location in his life. Matt put Melvin Potter, his former foe known as the Gladiator, in charge of Fogwell's (*Daredevil: Yellow* #1–6, 2001). Potter also owns a costume shop in the area.

Another prominent fixture in Daredevil stories is Josie's Bar & Grill, a tavern frequented by criminals and other lowlifes. It also receives frequent visits from Daredevil, who roughs up various patrons whenever he needs information about criminal activities in the vicinity. According to *Daredevil*, vol. 1, #161 (November 1979), the bar is located "in the shadow of the Brooklyn Bridge" in lower Manhattan. However, in *Daredevil*, vol. 2, #50 (October 2003), Murdock chooses Josie's Bar as the site where he proclaims himself the "kingpin" of Hell's Kitchen. Considering the tavern's prominent role in Daredevil stories, it makes more sense for it to be located in Hell's Kitchen. Josie's Bar also appears in the 2003 feature film *Daredevil*, based on the Marvel comic book. ✳

CENTRAL PARK

Fifty-ninth to One Hundred Tenth Streets, between Central Park West and Fifth Avenue

THE MOST FAMOUS URBAN park in the world, New York's Central Park provides a green oasis of beauty and tranquillity amidst the noise and bustle of Manhattan's streets and office buildings. In the Marvel Universe, however, Central Park is the battleground of choice for Super Heroes and Super Villains alike.

Central Park is not truly the nearly pristine natural environment it may seem at first glance. The team of landscape architect Frederick Law Olmsted and architect Calvert Vaux won an 1857 competition to design Central Park, and most of its 843 acres were artificially landscaped according to their design. Even the park's numerous bodies of water are man-made. Construction on Central Park was officially completed in 1873.

CENTRAL PARK

Among the famous landmarks in Central Park is Belvedere Castle, which was built in 1869 atop Vista Rock, the second-highest natural elevation within the park. The castle is the location of the U.S. Weather Bureau's Central Park meteorological observatory.

One of the park's biggest tourist attractions, the celebrated Central Park Zoo, officially started as the Central Park Menagerie in 1864. For most of the twentieth century the zoo housed large wild animals in enclosures that would be considered too small by today's more humane standards. In 1980 the Wildlife Conservation Society, which administers the Bronx Zoo, took over the Central Park Zoo as well and undertook a thorough renovation of the property and moved the larger animals to the more spacious Bronx venue. The Central Park Zoo reopened to the public in 1988. It is currently divided into three major sections: a children's zoo, featuring farm animals such as sheep and cows; a controlled-environment building housing animals from tropical rain forests; and exhibits of animals from arctic regions, including a penguin house and a large outdoor area for polar bears, who can safely endure the city's frigid winters. The sea-lion pool was redesigned and is still the zoo's central feature, attracting large crowds daily.

Each summer free performances of the plays of William Shakespeare (and sometimes of other playwrights) are staged by the New York Public Theater at Central Park's outdoor Delacorte Theatre. The Delacorte was named after the late George T. Delacorte Jr., who financed its construction and was the founder of the Dell Publishing Company, a major publisher of prose books, magazines, and comic books in the mid-twentieth century. New Yorkers are known to get in line early in the morning to secure the coveted free tickets to "Shakespeare in the Park," as the performances are known.

Other notable attractions in Central Park include Strawberry Fields, a memorial to John Lennon; the Lake, where

CENTRAL PARK

visitors can rent rowboats; and the Ramble, a thirty-eight-acre wild garden that is the bird-watching nexus of the park.

In the 1970s Central Park was a notoriously dangerous place to be after dark. In recent years, however, Central Park has become one of the safest urban parks in the United States.

In the Marvel Universe, on the other hand, it is a miracle that anyone ventures into Central Park during the day or the night. It is among the real-life locations most utilized as settings for Marvel stories, which means Super Hero battles take place there regularly.

Years ago, a criminal gang attempted to fake an invasion of New York City from outer space. Once the entire population had fled, the crooks reasoned (if reason had anything to do with this wild scheme), they could loot the entire city. From a phony construction site they established in Central Park, the gang projected an enormous floating head into the sky. Through loudspeakers that the crooks had set up around the city, the floating head proclaimed it was an invader from the planet Aqua Mentorius. But a small boy named Bruce, who was obviously smarter than most city officials, exposed the hoax, and the overreaching crooks were sent to jail (*Tales to Astonish* #8, March 1960).

Monsteroso, an alien infant over thirty-five feet tall, escaped from captivity in the American Museum of Natural History and wandered into nearby Central Park. With childish curiosity,

Monsteroso picked up and examined a lion and an elephant at the Central Park Zoo (*Amazing Adventures,* vol. 1, #5, October 1961).

In their first encounter, the original Kraven the Hunter stalked Spider-Man through a large, unnamed Manhattan park that is clearly meant to be Central Park (*Amazing Spider-Man* #15, August 1964).

The Leap-Frog, a criminal whose froglike costume gave him superhuman leaping abilities, was first bested by Daredevil in a battle in Central Park (*Daredevil,* vol. 1, #25, February 1967). Their next encounter also took place in Central Park shortly afterward (*Daredevil Annual* #1, September 1967).

Mowfus, the Creature from the Lost Lagoon is actually an amphibious alien from the planet Qu'on who has gone up against the Fantastic Four. On a visit to Earth, Mowfus and his mate hid within a cave beneath the Central Park Lake (*Fantastic Four,* vol. 1, #124–25, July–August 1972).

CENTRAL PARK

Shang-Chi, Master of Kung Fu, fought off a gang of muggers in Central Park, as the assassin Midnight secretly looked on (*Special Marvel Edition* #16, February 1974).

The most fateful event to occur in Central Park in Marvel history took place when U.S. marine captain Frank Castle brought his wife and young children to the park for a picnic. There they inadvertently witnessed a mob execution; the gangsters then gunned down every member of the Castle family. But Frank Castle survived and, driven by a fanatical need to avenge the deaths of his wife and children, has waged a one-man vigilante war on crime ever since as the Punisher (*Marvel Preview* #2, April 1975).

In real life, Marvel staffers used to play softball games in Central Park during the summer back in the 1970s. In the comics, Danny Rand (who was secretly the martial artist Iron Fist) accepted an invitation from new *Iron Fist* writer Chris Claremont to join in one of Marvel's Central Park games (*Marvel Premiere* #24, August 1975).

During one fierce battle there, a colossal monster called Braggadoom hurled the Thing through a stone wall in Central Park (*Marvel Two-in-One* #13, January 1976).

Dr. Arthur Nagan, alias Gorilla-Man, and the sorcerer Chondu, both members of the Headmen, overpowered and captured the Super Hero Nighthawk in Central Park as the first step of their plot to transplant Chondu's brain into Nighthawk's body (*Defenders,* vol. 1, #31, January 1976).

Brother Zed, a hypnotist who pretended to be a voodoo priest, attempted to perform a human sacrifice in Central Park, burying a victim alive, but was stopped by Daredevil (*Daredevil,* vol. 1, #130, February 1976).

To empower his new android, the Tri-Animan, the criminal mastermind known as the Masked Marauder stole three animals from the Central Park Zoo. Hence he was able to endow the Tri-Animan with the strength of a gorilla, the speed of a cheetah, and the vicious temperament of an alligator (*Werewolf by Night,* vol. 1, #42, January 1977).

Around that same time, Nova the Human Rocket fought a creature resembling the subterranean monarch Tyrannus, who was under the real Tyrannus's control (*Nova,* vol. 1, #15, January 1977).

Stegron the Dinosaur Man, a scientist who transformed himself into a humanoid dinosaur, battled both Spider-Man and the Lizard in the American Museum of Natural History. Escaping the museum, Stegron fled across the street into Central Park, but the winter cold slowed his movements, and he fell through the ice into Central Park's Lake (*Amazing Spider-*

Man #166, March 1977). Somehow reverting to human form, Stegron lived as a homeless man in Central Park until he finally regained his reptilian appearance.

A phony religious cult, the Legion of Light, publicly headed by Brother Power and Sister Sun, held a massive rally in Central Park. The Legion was actually controlled by the satanic Man-Beast, who used his mental powers to enslave the cultists (*Spectacular Spider-Man,* vol. 2, #12, November 1977).

Escaping from the island of his archenemy, Doctor Bong, Howard the Duck piloted the villain's *Flying Bonger* to New York City. The armed forces shot down this unidentified flying object, and Howard crash-landed in Central Park (*Howard the Duck,* vol. 1, #18, November 1977).

Peter Parker and his new girlfriend Cissy Ironwood were walking through Central Park when they were attacked, not by a mugger but by a werewolf. While Cissy was unconscious, Peter drove off their supernatural assailant (*Marvel Team-Up,* vol. 1, #80, April 1979).

The neofascist National Force, secretly controlled by the criminal psychiatrist Doctor Faustus, held a rally in Central Park, where Captain America's girlfriend, SHIELD agent Sharon Carter, fell victim to Faustus's mind-control gas (*Captain America,* vol. 1, #231–33, March–May 1979).

Seeking a new challenge, the members of the Gotham Game

Club decided to destroy the Hulk when he next turned up in New York City. Club member Earnest Stone drove a tank into Central Park and fired on the Hulk at Belvedere Castle. Stone should have known better: having smashed so many of the army's tanks for years, the Hulk made quick work of Stone's (*Incredible Hulk Annual* #9, 1980).

Around that same time, a fanatical costumed crusader named Status Quo staged a rally in Central Park, inciting a crowd to violence against anyone or anything different from the status quo. The mob then attacked an innocent bystander, Howard the Duck. Status Quo seized Howard and was about to hurl him from atop Belvedere Castle when Spider-Man came to the rescue. Howard pointed out that Status Quo's antifaddism was merely another fad, and the police took the rabble-rouser to jail (*Marvel Team-Up,* vol. 1, #96, August 1980).

After they escaped from the Hellfire Club mansion (which stands on Fifth Avenue, across from the park), the X-Men waged their first battle against Dark Phoenix in Central Park (*Uncanny X-Men* #135, August 1980).

A.I.M. (Advanced Idea Mechanics), a criminal organization of scientists, established a hidden base beneath Central Park (*Marvel Team-Up,* vol. 1, #102, February 1981).

Count Dracula once attempted to bring Storm, leader of the X-Men, under his control, but his plan to turn Storm into a vampire was foiled when the X-Men tracked them to his lair in Belvedere Castle (*Uncanny X-Men* #159, July 1982).

The virtually omnipotent being called the Beyonder created a strange alien construct that appeared in Central Park's fifteen-acre Sheep Meadow. The construct teleported itself and the Fantastic Four, Spider-Man, and many other heroes into outer space, where the heroes engaged in the first of the Beyonder's Secret Wars on his Battleworld. When the heroes finally returned to Sheep Meadow through the construct, Spider-Man was wearing his new black costume (*Amazing Spider-Man* #252, May 1984). The costume proved to be a living, alien creature that later merged with Eddie Brock to become the menace called Venom.

Hotspur, a sinister ghost from eighteenth-century England, took possession of the body of a modern New Yorker and did battle with the Defenders in Central Park (*Defenders,* vol. 1, #146–47, August–September 1985).

In one of the greatest coups of his centuries-long feud with his foster brother, Loki, god of evil, transformed the thunder god Thor into a frog. Thor discovered that he was able to communicate with other frogs and was led by a frog called Puddlegulp to a community of the amphibians living in Central Park. There, a pack of rats attacked and killed the frogs' ruler, King Glugwort. While a war ensued between the frogs and the rats, Thor led alligators up from New York's sewers, who then devoured the rat army. The frogs invited Thor to be their new king, but he declined, leaving Glugwort's daughter, Princess Greensong, as the new queen. Thor eventually recovered his enchanted hammer, which restored his true size and his godly powers, although he still looked like a frog for a short while thereafter (*Thor,* vol. 1, #364–65, February–March 1986). Later, Queen Greensong, Puddlegulp, and other frogs attended a performance of William Shakespeare's *The Comedy of Errors* at Central Park's Delacorte Theatre (*X-Men Annual* #10, 1986). Still later, the frogs of Central Park aided Doctor Strange after he had temporarily been transformed into a rat by his archenemy Dormammu (*Doctor Strange,* vol. 3, #2, January 1989).

A costumed figure calling himself the Super-Patriot held a rally in Central Park at which he denounced Captain America as being out of step with contemporary Americans. The Super-Patriot then staged a fight in which he defeated the Buckies, who claimed to be supporters of Captain America (*Captain America*, vol. 1, #323, November 1986). The Super-Patriot actually did take over the role of Captain America for a time, before assuming his current identity as the U.S. agent.

The Conspiracy, a cabal that sought to rule the world by tapping the mystical powers of the Bloodstone, had a secret headquarters beneath Central Park (*Captain America*, vol. 1, #358, September 1989).

Believing that he deserved to star in a Marvel comic more than she did, the insane costumed prankster Madcap confronted the She-Hulk in Central Park and tried to drive her literally crazy. Finally getting fed up with Madcap, She-Hulk simply tore out and crumpled up the comic book page Madcap was standing in! (*Sensational She-Hulk* #9, December 1989.)

When the alien Star-Stalker marauded through Central Park, the child Super Hero team Power Pack (who lived near the park) went after him. But it was the second Nova (Frankie Raye) who defeated him with her cosmic flame (*Power Pack*, vol. 1, #57, July 1990).

A swarm of microscopic insects from the Amazon jungles, which resembled a strange black cloud, devoured living animals at the Central Park Zoo and might have done the same to Spider-Man when he showed up, had he not been rescued by the Avengers (*Spectacular Spider-Man* #170, November 1990).

Intent on capturing a serial rapist, police detective Lynn Michaels made herself a target by jogging through Central Park. When the rapist attacked, the Punisher appeared, Michaels turned her gun on the vigilante, and the rapist fled, foiling Michaels's plan. However, the Punisher and Michaels became allies after that incident, and Lynn Michaels later became a costumed vigilante known as Lady Punisher (*Punisher War Zone* #7, September 1992).

The Night People of Zero Street, many of whom were once inmates of a mental asylum, now inhabit Zerotown, a shanty-town in caverns beneath Central Park (*Captain America*, vol. 1, #410–11, December 1992–January 1993). These may be the same caverns where the Conspiracy previously had its base.

The vampire hunter Blade, under the name Switchblade, waged a tremendous battle against Modred the Mystic, a sorcerer from the age of King Arthur, in Central Park (*Darkhold* #11, August 1993).

Around that same time in Central Park, Moon Knight, the Werewolf by Night, and Gambit took on eight supernatural creatures called the Hellbent (*Marc Spector, Moon Knight* #53, August 1993).

The Snakeroot, a cult of ninjas who serve a demonic being called the Beast, maintained their headquarters in underground catacombs beneath Belvedere Castle (*Daredevil*, vol. 1, #23, December 1993).

Captain America's two young protégés, Jack Flag and Free Spirit, were relaxing in Central Park when they discovered Madcap threatening to commit a suicide bombing. Jack was unable to prevent Madcap from setting off the bomb, but Madcap's ability to regenerate his body saved his life, and no one else was seriously harmed (*Captain America,* vol. 1, #442, August 1995).

Three costumed criminals, the Looter, Aura, and Override, battled "cyber-slayer" robots created by inventor Alistaire Smythe at the Central Park Children's Zoo (*Spectacular Scarlet Spider* #1, November 1995).

Onslaught was the malevolent psionic entity that resulted from combining the dark side of Charles Xavier's psyche with that of Magneto. Using reprogrammed Sentinel robots as his private army, Onslaught took control of the island of Manhattan and created a citadel for himself in Central Park. The Fantastic Four, the Avengers, the X-Men, and the Hulk banded together to attack Onslaught at this citadel. The Fantastic Four and the Avengers ultimately defeated Onslaught by plunging into his body, disrupting and dispersing the psychic energy of which it was composed (*Onslaught: Marvel Universe,* October 1996).

During an expedition in the Canadian Arctic, scientist Michael Fleet was transformed into the man-eating monster called the Wendigo. The creature was captured and placed aboard an aircraft that flew over New York City. The Wendigo broke free, escaped into Central Park, and killed a number of people at the Central Park Zoo. Both Spider-Man and the second Ghost Rider hunted the Wendigo down, and the Ghost Rider used his "penance stare" to reduce the creature into submission (*Marvel Fanfare,* vol. 2, #2–3, October–November 1996).

The Lady of the Lake is the mysterious supernatural figure who presented King Arthur with the sword Excalibur. She rose from the Central Park Lagoon to appear to Dane Whitman, the modern successor to King Arthur's champion, the Black Knight (*Heroes for Hire* #2, August 1997).

The Elements of Doom, artificial creatures that are each composed of one pure element, launched a terrorist assault on Central Park, only to meet resistance from Daredevil, Spider-Man, the New Warriors, and the Thunderbolts (*Thunderbolts,* vol. 1, #8, November 1997).

Mob family leader Ma Gnucci and her gang pursued the Punisher into Central Park, where Ma was severely mauled (but not killed) by the polar bears in the Central Park Zoo (*Punisher,* vol. 5, #4, July 2000).

Norman Osborn, alias the Green Goblin, murdered *Daily Bugle* reporter Terri Kidder for her investigation of mysterious disappearances at Os Corp, and disposed of her corpse in the Central Park Reservoir (*The Pulse* #1–5, April–August 2004).

For a time the self-appointed protector of Central Park was Squirrel Girl, a teenager with mutant powers resembling the abilities of squirrels (*Great Lakes Avengers* #2, July 2005). Not only can she communicate with real squirrels, but she even has a bushy, prehensile tail. Once Squirrel Girl aided the Thing when he battled the two-headed Bi-Beast in Central Park (*Thing,* vol. 2, #8, August 2006). However, Squirrel Girl abandoned Central Park when she became a member of the Great Lakes Avengers, based in Wisconsin.

The sentient robot Elektro once took Roberta, the Fantastic Four's robot receptionist, to Central Park on a date. Shortly after, the ancient dragon Fin Fang Foom, having been reduced to human size through a rehabilitation program for giant monsters, played a friendly game of chess with Reed Richards in the park (*Marvel Monsters: Fin Fang Four* #1, December 2005).

After being attacked in Central Park, a young woman named Kate Bishop studied boxing, jujitsu, archery, and other methods of combat so that she would never be a victim again. Eventually she joined the Young Avengers, becoming the new Hawkeye (*Young Avengers Special* #1, 2006).

In the alternate reality of the *House of M* limited series (2005), Magneto led mutantkind in a war against the rest of the human race. Magneto's climactic battle against the humans and their Sentinel robots took place in Central Park. A monument commemorating the mutants' victory was subsequently erected there. *

EMBASSIES/CONSULATES

Latverian Embassy, Park Avenue in the East Sixties

Symkarian Embassy, Madison Avenue and East Fifty-third Street

Wakandan Embassy, Madison Avenue in the East Seventies

THERE ARE NUMEROUS NATIONS on Marvel-Earth that have no counterparts in the real world. Three of the most important of these imaginary countries—Latveria, Symkaria, and Wakanda—have established official offices on Manhattan's Upper East Side. In the comics these offices are referred to as embassies. But, assuming that all three countries have ambassadors stationed in Washington, D.C., as well, then their New York offices should actually be considered consulates.

Many nations of the world have established consulates in New York City. A consulate is an office for official representatives of a foreign nation, who are stationed there to promote good relations between their country and the host nation, and to provide aid to their countrymen who are visiting or living in the host nation.

These consulates are familiarly known as embassies, although the word *embassy* is properly applied to a foreign nation's principal office in a host nation. Hence, a foreign nation would have its embassy in Washington, D.C., the capital of the United States, but might have a consulate in New York City, its financial capital, to promote trade.

The Latverian, Symkarian, and Wakandan "embassies" or consulates are legally regarded as the territory of their respective nations.

This makes the Latverian consulate potentially the most dangerous place in New York City. Latveria, a tiny pocket kingdom in the Balkan Mountains of Eastern Europe, is ruled by Doctor Victor von Doom, one of Marvel's greatest Super Villains. Von

Doom has extraordinary scientific genius, rivaled only by that of his archenemy, Reed Richards of the Fantastic Four. Doctor Doom has invented advanced weaponry that makes Latveria a threat to the rest of the world, even to a superpower such as the United States. Indeed, Doom has undertaken repeated attempts at world conquest.

Rather than provoke his wrath, the United States has granted Doctor Doom diplomatic immunity as the chief representative of his nation. Hence, Doom can enter the United States at will and has used the Latverian consulate in New York as a base of operations. For example, in *Fantastic Four Annual* #2 (1964), Doom engaged Richards in a literal battle of wills, using a device called an encephalo-gun in an effort to determine who had the superior intellect.

In *Fantastic Four,* vol. 1, #287 (February 1986), Doom, disguised as the Invincible Man, persuaded the Super Heroines the Invisible Woman, She-Hulk, and the Wasp to help him attack the Latverian consulate. Once inside, Doom captured the Invisible Woman and, in the following issue, bested the other Super Heroines, Reed Richards, and the Human Torch.

Doctor Doom has stationed fifty of his "servo-guard" robot soldiers within the Latverian consulate to deal with intruders.

Symkaria is a tiny pocket kingdom that borders Latveria. Symkaria's principal source of foreign income is Silver Sable International, a mercenary organization headed by the glamorous adventuress Silver Sable. Decades ago, her father founded the Wild Pack, a team of soldiers who tracked down and apprehended Nazi war criminals. Since few such criminals are still at large, Silver Sable redirected the Wild Pack toward profit-making ventures. For a steep price, Silver Sable International accepts assignments from nations and private companies to hunt down and apprehend criminals and to recover stolen property.

When she is in the United States, Silver Sable and her Wild Pack use the Symkarian consulate in New York City as their base of operations. Silver and her consulate made their first appearances in *Amazing Spider-Man,* vol. 1, #265 (June 1985).

Wakanda is an African nation ruled by a king, T'Challa, who has adopted the traditional ceremonial costume of the Black Panther. As the Black Panther he has operated as a Super Hero, both on his own and as a member of the Avengers. The Black Panther and Wakanda first appeared in *Fantastic Four*, vol. 1, #52, July 1966.

Wakanda is the only place on Earth where Wakandan vibranium, a metal that fell to Earth as a meteorite and that absorbs sonic vibrations, can be found. By selling small amounts of vibranium to the outside world, Wakanda became a prosperous and highly technologically advanced nation.

Wakanda established a consulate in Manhattan, where T'Challa resides when he is in New York City. Recently, T'Challa wed Storm of the X-Men. During the Civil War between Super Heroes, the Wakandan consulate was demolished (*Black Panther*, vol. 4, #25, April 2007). On the invitation of Reed Richards, T'Challa has established a temporary Wakandan consulate in the Baxter Building in midtown Manhattan, while a new consulate is being constructed. ✸

FRICK COLLECTION/ AVENGERS MANSION

Seventieth Street between Fifth and Madison Avenues

ONE OF THE MOST important landmarks in Marvel New York is Avengers Mansion, the headquarters and home for "Earth's mightiest heroes." In Marvel continuity, the mansion belonged to Howard and Maria Stark, the wealthy parents of industrialist and inventor Tony Stark. Years after his parents' deaths, Tony secretly became the armored Super Hero Iron Man and a founding member of the Avengers. Stark donated the mansion to the Avengers for use as their home base. The expenses of running the mansion were paid by the Maria Stark Foundation.

Most readers of *Avengers* over the decades are probably unaware that Avengers Mansion is based on a real mansion that they can visit on Manhattan's Fifth Avenue. This is the palatial building that now houses the museum known as the Frick Collection.

Avengers co-creator Stan Lee explained in an interview for the Travel Channel, "There was a mansion called the Frick Museum [*sic*] that I used to walk past. I sort of modeled [Avengers Mansion] after that. Beautiful, big, so impressive [a] building, right on Fifth Avenue."

The Frick Collection's actual address is 1 East Seventieth Street, but Avengers Mansion's address is 809 Fifth Avenue. This probably means that the Avengers Mansion entrance faces Fifth Avenue and Central Park, whereas the Frick's doors are on Seventieth Street.

Henry Clay Frick (1849–1919) made his fortune in manufacturing steel and used that wealth to build his own extraordinary collection of art. In 1910 he bought the site at Fifth Avenue and Seventieth Street and started construction of his New York mansion. Frick died not long after, in 1919. Four years after the death of his widow, Adelaide, in 1931, the mansion was opened to the public as an art museum. Despite its relatively small size, the Frick Collection probably contains more masterpieces of painting per square foot than any other museum. Among the masters represented are Rembrandt, Titian, Van Dyck, Vermeer, and Whistler.

Avengers Mansion first appeared in the team's second issue (*Avengers*, vol. 1, #2, November 1963), and their butler, Edwin Jarvis, made his debut in *Tales of Suspense* #59 (November

1964). Jarvis had been Tony Stark's butler, and he agreed to serve the Avengers in the same capacity.

Jarvis's duties eventually expanded far beyond those of a conventional butler. The Avengers extensively remodeled the interior of the mansion to suit the requirements of a Super Hero team. Hence, Jarvis also oversaw the mansion's security and communication systems and the maintenance of their aerial vehicles and computers.

For security reasons, Avengers Mansion was surrounded on three sides by a twelve-foot-high wall of steel and concrete, with a steel fence along the Fifth Avenue side. The exterior of the building and the grounds contained sophisticated surveillance devices. Nonetheless, the Avengers felt safe in utilizing the garden and patio behind the mansion, which was further screened from public view by trees.

The only part of the mansion that was sometimes open to members of the public for social functions was the first floor. This was also the location of the public conference room, where the Avengers held press conferences, as well as the Avengers' dining room, their library, and Jarvis's private quarters.

Avengers serving full-time active duty at the mansion were invited to live on the second floor, which contained eight different bedrooms. Any bedroom not occupied by a full-time member could be used by an Avengers reservist. The second floor remained virtually unchanged from when Howard and Maria Stark lived there.

In contrast, the third floor, the topmost, was converted into a hangar for the Avengers' supersonic VTOL (vertical takeoff and landing) aircraft, the Quinjets. One of the exterior walls would open to permit Quinjets to take off or land.

Howard Stark had constructed three basement levels beneath the mansion and used the lowest of them as a private testing and storage area for the weapon systems his company developed. The Avengers greatly expanded and renovated these basement levels to serve as their combat headquarters.

The first basement level held the Avengers' gymnasium, their medical facilities, and a "combat simulation room," similar to the original version of the X-Men's Danger Room, which they used for training.

Beneath that basement was Sub-Basement Level One, the location of the Assembly Room, where the Avengers' strategy meetings were held. Comparable to the White House's underground Situation Room, the Assembly Room, with its heavily reinforced walls, was considered the most secure location in the entire complex. This level also held the Avengers' state-of-the-art computer system.

Finally, the lowest level, Sub-Basement Level Two, included storage areas, a weapons-test area left over from Howard

Stark's days, and a docking area for the Avengers' submarine, which could exit through a passage to the East River.

Even more than Manhattan's iconic locations such as the Empire State Building, Avengers Mansion was a prime target for supercriminals and has been destroyed many times over in Marvel's history.

The first instance of wholesale destruction occurred after Baron Helmut Zemo and his Masters of Evil captured Avengers Mansion. The mansion's floors aboveground were demolished in the Avengers' successful battle to take the site back from the Masters (*Avengers,* vol. 1, #273–77, November 1986–March 1987). The wreckage was cleared away, and the site was temporarily converted into Avengers Park, while the team set up a new headquarters on Hydrobase, a floating artificial island off the New York City coast.

In time the Avengers built a new headquarters on the mansion site, but it bore no resemblance whatsoever to the original Stark mansion. However, this building was in turn demolished by transdimensional menaces called the Gatherers. Then Ute, a member of the alien race of Watchers, transported an alternate-reality version of Avengers Mansion, identical to the original, to this site as a gift to the Super Heroes (*Avengers,* vol. 1, #375, June 1994).

But this version of Avengers Mansion was devastated

beyond repair in the dreadful battles chronicled in the "Avengers Disassembled" story line in 2004 (*Avengers,* vol. 1, #500–03, 2004). At that point, Tony Stark decided that he could not afford to rebuild the mansion once again.

As a result, the Avengers are headquartered in Avengers Tower, as of *New Avengers* #1 (November 2004). Formerly known as Stark Tower, it is a ninety-three-floor skyscraper built and designed by Tony Stark, who previously used the topmost three floors as his private residence. Stark has since turned these floors over to the Avengers.

Various members of the Avengers live in the Tower, including Spider-Man, who moved in along with his wife, Mary Jane, and his aunt May. Besides residential quarters, the new headquarters house a Quinjet hangar, gymnasium, and medical and laboratory facilities. The walls of the building are composed of concrete reinforced with vibranium, a metal that absorbs vibrations, making them nearly indestructible.

The Watchtower, the headquarters of another member of the Avengers, the Sentry, stands at the pinnacle of Avengers Tower.

The exact location of Stark Tower in Manhattan has not been established at this time.

As for Avengers Mansion, it seems unlikely that it is gone for good. Traditions often eventually reassert themselves in Marvel history. And so one day, perhaps Avengers Mansion will be rebuilt, in a form resembling the original design based on the Frick Collection.

In the alternate continuity of Marvel's Ultimate line, the original Avengers are known as the Ultimates, and they are based in the Triskelion, a high-tech complex that the security agency SHIELD erected on an artificial island in Upper New York Bay. The Triskelion is named after its main building, a tower with three wings. Instead of a mansion, the Triskelion is more like a military base, with barracks for SHIELD troops, hangars and airstrips for fighter jets, docks for naval craft, and holding facilities for superpowered captives. The Triskelion first appeared in *Ultimates* #3 (May 2002). ✳

SOLOMON R. GUGGENHEIM MUSEUM
East Eighty-ninth Street at Fifth Avenue

THE SOLOMON R. GUGGENHEIM Museum is the last major building designed by Frank Lloyd Wright, who was arguably the greatest American architect of the twentieth century. The building's distinctive exterior and unique design are as famous as the works of art housed within. Visitors to the museum ascend a gallery that spirals from the rotunda, around and around, ever upward to the top of the building. The rotunda, a vast, nearly empty space, is named after Ronald O. Perelman, former owner of Marvel Comics and the former president of the museum's board of trustees.

Founded in 1937 by philanthropist Solomon R. Guggenheim to showcase modern, abstract art, the institution was originally called the Museum of Non-Objective Painting. The Wright-designed building opened in 1959. Not only has the Guggenheim remained one of New York City's leading art museums, it has also spawned branches around the world, notably in Bilbao, Spain.

The real Guggenheim Museum has never hosted an exhibit related to toys; nevertheless, the Super Villain team of Mr. Hyde and the Cobra once broke into the Guggenheim to steal toys that were valuable collector's items on behalf of their ally the Jester (*Daredevil,* vol. 1, #61, February 1970).

Years later, the Absorbing Man and his partner Titania attempted to steal a life-size golden bull that was on display at the Guggenheim (*Thor* #447–48, May–June 1992).

In an alternate reality, Conan the Barbarian was somehow transported to modern New York City. When Conan saw a picture of the Guggenheim Museum, something told him that the building might hold the key to his returning home. He ascended to the top of the building—foiling museum looters on the way—where he was struck by a bolt of mystical lightning, which did indeed return him to his own time (*What If,* vol. 1, #13, February 1979). ✴

ONLY A FEW BLOCKS DOWN FIFTH AVENUE FROM AVENGERS MANSION STANDS A BUILDING THAT -- LIKE THE VAN-- IS FAR LESS INNOCENT THAN IT APPEARS.

THIS IS THE LEGENDARY HELLFIRE CLUB.

HELLFIRE CLUB

Fifth Avenue and East Sixty-sixth Street

THE PALATIAL HELLFIRE CLUB mansion on Manhattan's East Side is the epicenter for the elite of New York City society. It is home to a highly exclusive organization consisting of members of the world's wealthiest families, the heads of powerful corporations, and leading political figures. The Hellfire Club's annual gala is the foremost event in Manhattan high society. Since the Hellfire Club dates back to England in the 1700s, many members wear eighteenth-century costumes to the gala and the club's other social events. To be invited to join the Hellfire Club is a sign of ultimate success in the worlds of business, politics, and high society.

Unknown to the world at large, and even to the majority of its membership, the prestigious Hellfire Club also has a secret Inner Circle, which seeks world domination through political and economic means.

In the real world, various societies were known as Hellfire Clubs in eighteenth-century England. The most famous of these was founded by Sir Francis Dashwood in London in 1746 and became notorious for sexually risqué activities and pagan rituals.

According to Marvel history, in the 1770s Sir Patrick Clemens and Lady Diana Knight emigrated to New York, where they founded the American chapter of the Hellfire Club in an abandoned church on the site of the present mansion.

The Hellfire Club's first important and most infamous role in Marvel history is the part that the Inner Circle played in the "Dark Phoenix Saga" (*Uncanny X-Men* #129–37, January–September 1980). At that time the Inner Circle was dominated by superhuman mutants, led by its Black King, Sebastian Shaw. Petitioning for admission to the Inner Circle, Jason Wyngarde, the mutant called Mastermind, sought to prove his worthiness by mesmerizing Jean Grey, a member of the X-Men. Mastermind's psychic brainwashing compelled Grey to become the Inner Circle's new Black Queen. Aided by Grey, the Inner Circle captured other members of the X-Men and held them prisoner behind the scenes during one of the club's lavish parties. However, Grey was able to overcome Mastermind's psychic control and helped free the X-Men, leading to a melee that spilled over into the ballroom, throwing the party into chaos.

The X-Men escaped, but Mastermind's mental manipulation of Jean eventually triggered her transformation into the sinister Dark Phoenix.

"Dark Phoenix Saga" writer Chris Claremont established in *Uncanny X-Men* #132 (April 1980) that the Hellfire Club mansion was "four blocks" down Fifth Avenue from Avengers Mansion. Since Avengers Mansion is at Seventieth Street and Fifth Avenue, this puts the Hellfire Club mansion at Sixty-sixth Street. Unlike Avengers Mansion, however, the Hellfire Club mansion does not appear to be based on a specific real-world building. ✳

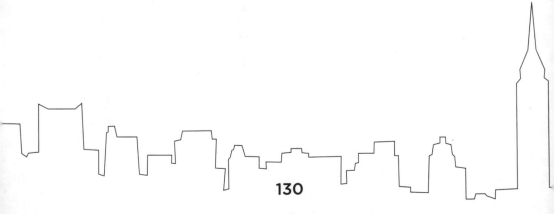

METROPOLITAN MUSEUM OF ART

Fifth Avenue between Eightieth and Eighty-fourth Streets

ONE OF THE WORLD'S largest and foremost art museums, the Metropolitan Museum of Art holds a vast, encyclopedic collection ranging from ancient-Egyptian artifacts to contemporary American painting, photography, and video. The Met displays works by such giants as Cézanne, Degas, Matisse, Monet, Picasso, Raphael, Rembrandt, Rubens, Titian, van Gogh, and Vermeer, as well as artwork from ancient Greece and Rome, China and Japan, Africa and the South Pacific. Among its most popular exhibits are the ancient Egyptian Temple of Dendur and the iconic American painting *Washington Crossing the Delaware.*

Founded in 1870, the Metropolitan moved to its present site within Central Park, along Fifth Avenue, in 1880. The original Central Park building, designed in Gothic Revival style, still stands as the core of the museum. The museum's magnificent beaux arts facade and entrance along Fifth Avenue, designed by Richard Morris Hunt, were finished in 1926. The complex was vastly expanded through the building of new wings in the late 1970s and 1980s. It is one of the most popular tourist attractions in New York, welcoming over 5 million visitors a year.

One might think that with its wealth of treasures, the Metropolitan would be a prime target for New York's superpowerful crooks. But the Met must have an anti–Super Villain security system that is state-of-the-art, because the museum rarely turns up in Marvel stories.

One theft that nearly succeeded was actually an inside job. Arthur Reynolds worked for the Metropolitan as an art restorer. Reynolds learned that one of his colleagues at the Met, Lawrence Chesney, who had recently died, had been a costumed criminal named Copperhead. Stealing Chesney's costume, Reynolds became the new Copperhead, murdered one of the Met's curators, and attempted to steal an enormous urn from the museum. Reynolds was thwarted by the White Tiger, a Super Hero, and the Human Fly, a costumed stuntman, and fell off a pier into the Hudson River and apparently drowned when they pursued him (*Human Fly* #8–9, April–May 1978).

Soon afterward, another costumed villain, also called the Fly, attempted to burglarize the museum, but was foiled by

Spider-Man. This Fly escaped, only to be caught by the New York City police (*Amazing Spider-Man*, vol. 1, #193, June 1979).

Within the Metropolitan's impressive Egyptian collection was the Crown of Hathor, an ancient object of mystical power. Gamal Hassan, the curator of the Met's Egyptian department, was the descendant of the evil Egyptian sorcerer Nephrus. Hassan stole the crown as part of his plan to become the host of Nephrus' spirit. But the Thing, Nephrus' ancient enemy the Living Mummy, and Met assistant curator Lillian Templeworth together defeated Nephrus, causing Hassan's body to crumble into dust (*Marvel Two-in-One* #95, January 1983).

The Met's most memorable appearance in Marvel history also involved spirits from the past and took place in *Marvel Team-Up* #79 (March 1979). The Met's curators had been unable to identify a mysterious necklace that predated the earliest known civilization. The necklace actually belonged to Kulan Gath, a sinister sorcerer from the legendary Hyborian Age, who was an enemy of Conan the Barbarian and his swordswoman ally, Red Sonja.

On the night of the winter solstice, Gath's spirit induced a museum security guard to don the necklace. Gath then took mental possession of the guard, transforming his body into a duplicate of Gath's own.

But, unfortunately for Gath, the Met also had in its collection the sword of Red Sonja. When Mary Jane Watson touched the sword, she was magically turned into a double of Red Sonja, whose spirit took possession of MJ's body. Together Spider-Man and Red Sonja defeated Kulan Gath. Mary Jane and the guard returned to normal, and Spider-Man dropped the enchanted necklace into New York Bay off the coast of Staten Island. ✳

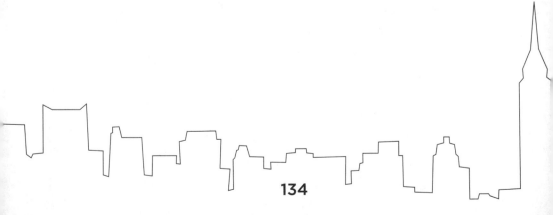

NELSON AND MURDOCK

LAWYER MATT MURDOCK, WHO is also the costumed crime-fighter Daredevil, and his friend from Columbia Law School, Franklin "Foggy" Nelson, founded the most celebrated law firm in Marvel history. The offices of Nelson and Murdock are located in the East Sixties between Fifth Avenue and Madison Avenue.

Foggy Nelson lives nearby, in an apartment on Park Avenue in the East Seventies. When he served as New York City's district attorney, he worked at One Hogan Place in lower Manhattan. This is where the New York DA's office is located in real life, so presumably Marvel's fictional DA's, such as Blake Tower, worked there, too.

Matt Murdock lived in a town house on Lexington Avenue in the East Sixties, until his enemy, the Kingpin, blew it up. Murdock subsequently moved to Hell's Kitchen on the West Side, a neighborhood under Daredevil's protection.

SHIELD HEADQUARTERS

Secret Headquarters: East Fifty-ninth Street and Madison Avenue
Public Headquarters: Midtown on the East Side

SHIELD IS AN INTERNATIONAL counterterrorism, intelligence, and security agency that combats such threats to world peace as the subversive organization Hydra. Its initials originally stood for Supreme Headquarters, International Espionage Law-Enforcement Division; in 1991 the title was changed to Strategic Hazard Intervention, Espionage and Logistics Directorate. The man most associated with the organization is Nick Fury, the American war hero who has been SHIELD's most effective director.

SHIELD's primary headquarters is its immense Heli-Carrier, which is continually in flight, remaining in no one location. SHIELD does, however, maintain offices on Manhattan's East Side to be able to deal with the public.

SHIELD also has a secret underground base beneath the streets of Manhattan. Agents gain access through a barbershop near Fifty-ninth Street and Madison Avenue, staffed by SHIELD employees (*Strange Tales*, vol. 1, #136, September 1965). When another agent enters, they can activate a device to fog the windows of the shop sufficiently to prevent passersby from seeing inside. The agent sits in one of the barber chairs, and the staff activates a system that lowers the chair beneath the floor, into the secret base below.

The agents who work in the shop—Sam, Slim, and an unnamed woman—are prepared to act against any enemy intruders. They can even quickly disguise the barbershop as a hardware store to thwart adversaries who might be looking for it. But they presumably spend most of their time attending to actual customers looking for a haircut and a manicure. ✳

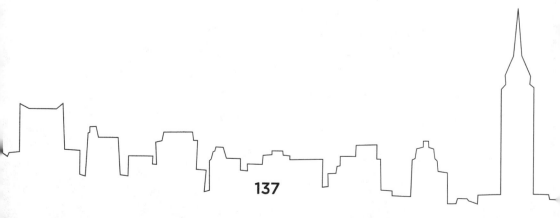

AMERICAN MUSEUM OF NATURAL HISTORY

Manhattan Square, Seventy-seventh to Eighty-first Streets between Central Park West and Columbus Avenue

THE AMERICAN MUSEUM of Natural History is one of the greatest museums of the natural sciences in the world. It is most renowned for its extraordinary collections of fossil skeletons of dinosaurs and other prehistoric animals, which now take up nearly the entire fourth floor of the museum. Rivaling the fossils in fame are the museum's celebrated dioramas displaying stuffed specimens of African, North American, Asian, and Oceanic wildlife in re-creations of their natural habitats, as well as the ninety-four-foot-long replica of a blue whale, which hangs in the Milstein Hall of Ocean Life.

Founded in 1869, the museum was originally housed in the State Arsenal building in Central Park. In 1874 construction began at the museum's current site in Manhattan Park, opposite Central Park on the Upper West Side. The first part of the museum complex, built in a Gothic style, opened in 1877. J. Cleaveland Cady designed the museum's southern facade, along Seventy-seventh Street, in a neo-Romanesque style that resembles a storybook castle, complete with towers and turrets. Later, architect John Russell Pope designed the Theodore Roosevelt Memorial, which honors the twenty-sixth president and serves as the museum's main entrance on Central Park West. Created in a beaux arts style to resemble a vast Roman basilica, the memorial entrance opened in 1936. The centerpiece of the memorial is a cast of a skeleton of an enormous barosaurus, rearing on its hind legs to defend its young from an attacking allosaurus.

The Hayden Planetarium, on the museum's north side, opened in 1935, but recently underwent a major renovation and in 2000 reopened as the Rose Center for Earth and Space. Designed by James Stewart Polshek, the Rose Center contains a gigantic sphere, housing the new planetarium, within a seven-story glass cube. It is considered one of the most stunning examples of contemporary architecture in New York City.

One of the most famous scientists in the museum's history

was the explorer and paleontologist Roy Chapman Andrews, who is considered one of the inspirations for George Lucas's character Indiana Jones. Marvel published the comic book *The Further Adventures of Indiana Jones* from 1983 into 1986.

As one of New York's best-loved cultural attractions, the museum has cropped up in Marvel history from time to time. A gigantic alien infant, which was at least thirty-five feet tall, inadvertently crash-landed on Earth in Africa and subsequently fell into a comatose state. Thought to be dead, the creature, dubbed Monsteroso, was transported to New York and put on display at the American Museum of Natural History. Abruptly reviving, Monsteroso, confused by his new surroundings, broke out of the museum and wandered through the city, creating panic. Finally, Monsteroso's even more enormous parents arrived in a starship and retrieved their lost child (*Amazing Adventures*, vol. 1, #5, October 1961).

In the first story in which Spider-Man encountered his enemy the Lizard, Peter Parker went to an unidentified New York City museum to do research on reptiles. The tyrannosaurus skeleton in the background of one panel indicates it was the American Museum of Natural History (*Amazing Spider-Man* #6, November 1963). The skeleton was stationary back then—but just wait.

The Man-Thing, a supernatural creature that inhabits a Florida swamp, was captured by Dr. Dane Gavin and put on exhibit at the American Museum of Natural History. This monster was a lot smaller than Monsteroso, so perhaps the museum staff thought they could hold on to this one. Not surprisingly, they were wrong. Visitors to the museum were frightened by the creature's grotesque appearance, causing the empathic Man-Thing to go berserk and break out of the museum. Dr. Gavin and Carolyn Schist, the daughter of a deceased enemy of the creature, ultimately subdued the creature and wisely returned the Man-Thing to his swamp (*Giant-Size Man-Thing* #2, November 1974).

Apparently not learning from its past mistakes, the museum later exhibited yet another colossal comatose alien, this time called the Monolith, which had been found buried on the South Seas island of Muara. Two residents of Muara traveled to New York and convinced the Avengers to help them return the Monolith to its rightful home. Luckily for the people of New York, the Monolith did not awaken until after it had safely been returned to Muara (*Avengers*, vol. 1, #179, January 1979).

Dr. Vincent Stegron combined dinosaur DNA with his own to transform himself into Stegron the Dinosaur Man. Using a "retro-generation ray," Stegron once brought dinosaur skeletons at the American Museum of Natural History to life (*Amazing*

Spider-Man #165–66, February–March 1977). Returning to the scene of the crime, Stegron subsequently used the museum as his base in a failed scheme to transform the people of Manhattan into an army of "dinosaur men" like himself (*The Lethal Foes of Spider-Man* #102, September–October 1993). Still later, Stegron sent the Rock of Life to the museum, where its radiation began to devolve the people of Manhattan into an animalistic state (*Sensational Spider-Man*, vol. 3, #26–27, July–August 2006). On all three of these occasions, Stegron was thwarted by his nemesis Spider-Man.

Ulysses Bloodstone was a prehistoric man who was endowed with near immortality by the mystical Bloodgem and became an adventurer and soldier of fortune. After Bloodstone finally met his demise, Baron Helmut Zemo located his skeleton at the American Museum of Natural History, an appropriate resting place considering his origins (*Captain America* #358, October 1989).

Dr. Buck Mitty was an entomologist, a scientist who studies insects, who used his knowledge to become the costumed criminal Humbug. Seeking to steal the Cheops Scarab from the "New York Museum of Natural History," Humbug battled Spider-Man. Ironically, Humbug ignominiously fell through a floor that had been weakened by termites and knocked himself out (*Spider-Man: Bug Stops Here* #1, 1994).

Doctor Yesterday, a mad scientist who could manipulate time, was yet another villain who regarded the museum as the perfect base of operations. But when the doctor got there, he ended up battling the New Warriors and Slapstick, who, by some improbable coincidence, were all visiting the museum that day. Demonstrating a lack of originality, Doctor Yesterday animated the same tyrannosaurus skeleton that Stegron had once brought to life and sent it to battle the young Super Heroes (*Marvel Comics Presents* #159, July 1994).

The former Russian spy Natasha Romanova, the Black Widow, was seemingly (but not actually) assassinated at the museum by her successor, Yelena Belova, with whom she had temporarily switched bodies (*Black Widow*, vol. 2, #1, January 2001).

In the movie *Spider-Man 2* (2004), the benefit for the Science Library is held at the Rose Center for Earth and Space. This is where Mary Jane Watson's engagement to John Jameson is announced, and Peter Parker is present to take pictures for the *Daily Bugle*. ✳

COLUMBUS CIRCLE

Intersection of Broadway, Central Park West, Central Park South, and Eighth Avenue

A STATUE OF CHRISTOPHER Columbus stands atop a monument at the center of this large traffic circle at the southwest corner of Central Park. Frederick Law Olmsted, one of the designers of Central Park, first conceived of the circle as an entrance to the park. It was finally completed in 1905 and is considered the first traffic circle established in the United States.

Columbus Circle is the former site of the New York Coliseum, which was once the city's leading convention center (and even hosted comics conventions). The Coliseum was torn down in

2000, and the new Time Warner Center, world headquarters of Time Warner Inc. as well as the home of many upscale stores and restaurants, was erected in its place. New York's principal convention venue is now the Jacob K. Javits Convention Center (also the home of comics conventions) in the West Thirties along the Hudson River.

The Coliseum is the "New York Convention Center" where the New Populist Party held its convention to nominate a candidate for president. They asked Captain America to run, but he appeared at the convention only to turn them down (*Captain America*, vol. 1, #250, October 1980).

Storm of the X-Men once battled Count Dracula in the sky above Columbus Circle. During their fight they crashed through the windows of the Top of the Park restaurant atop the Gulf & Western building on Columbus Circle (*Uncanny X-Men* #159, July 1982). The restaurant closed to the public in 1988 and was converted into a private banquet facility. ✳

COLUMBUS CIRCLE

LINCOLN CENTER FOR THE PERFORMING ARTS

West Sixty-second to West Sixty-fifth Streets between Amsterdam Avenue and Columbus Avenue

BUILT IN THE 1960S, Lincoln Center for the Performing Arts is a complex of buildings that house many of New York City's— and the world's—leading cultural institutions. Among them is the Metropolitan Opera, America's foremost opera company, which is housed in the enormous opera house that is Lincoln Center's centerpiece. The New York Philharmonic orchestra plays in Avery Fisher Hall, on the right of the Lincoln Center plaza. On the left, the New York State Theater is the base for both the New York City Ballet and the New York City Opera. Among the other institutions based at Lincoln Center are the Juilliard School for the arts, the Film Society of Lincoln Center, Lincoln Center Theater, and the New York Public Library for the Performing Arts.

In addition to the resident New York companies, performing arts organizations from around the world regularly perform at the different venues in Lincoln Center. Ororo Munroe (Storm) and Kitty Pryde (Shadowcat) of the X-Men are both ballet aficionados, and X-Men physical trainer Stevie Hunter is a former ballet dancer. All three have attended performances at Lincoln Center. For example, in *Uncanny X-Men* #145 (May 1981), Ororo and Stevie attend a performance at the Metropolitan Opera House by Britain's Royal Ballet.

Thinking they had brought about the deaths of Wolverine and the Black Cat, the villains Arcade and the White Rabbit decided to celebrate by attending a performance at the Met. But they never got there, since Wolverine and the Black Cat weren't dead after all and turned up angry at Arcade's home (*Claws* #3, December 2006).

Apart from Arcade and the White Rabbit, Super Villains seem to have little interest in Lincoln Center. The Ghost Rider once pursued a vampire called Night Terror there (*Ghost Rider*

Annual #1, 1993), but otherwise Lincoln Center is an area of relative serenity amid Manhattan's continual superhuman battles.

The one major exception to this rule occurred when the Wrecking Crew, a team of superhumanly strong criminals, attempted to demolish the complex to lure their old enemy Thor into their clutches. The trick worked, since Thor showed up, but he quickly overpowered the Crew members, and the center remained mostly intact (*Thor* #304, February 1981). Considering that Thor, under the name Donner, is a character in Richard Wagner's opera cycle *The Ring of the Nibelung,* it seems appropriate that he was the Metropolitan Opera's savior. ✳

COLUMBIA UNIVERSITY
Main campus: 116th Street between Broadway and Amsterdam Avenue

ONE OF THE EIGHT universities of the Ivy League, Columbia University is probably the best-known institution of higher learning in New York City.

The school was founded in 1754 as King's College and received a royal charter from Britain's King George II. Following the American Revolution, the school was rechristened Columbia College in 1784. In 1896 the school was renamed again, as Columbia University, and moved to its present main campus (formerly the site of the Bloomingdale Insane Asylum!) in the Morningside Heights neighborhood uptown.

The Columbia University campus was designed by McKim, Mead and White, the leading American architectural firm of that period. Its centerpiece is Low Memorial Library, a domed building that was constructed in 1895. Despite its name, Low Library has long been the university's main administration building. Upon its steps is another of Columbia's symbols, the statue *Alma Mater,* created by sculptor Daniel Chester French, who designed the colossal statue of Abraham Lincoln for Washington's Lincoln Memorial.

Columbia's Graduate School of Journalism administers the famous Pulitzer Prizes, named after newspaper mogul Joseph

149

Pulitzer (one of whose newspaper, *The New York World*, published the first color comic strip, *The Yellow Kid*).

Alexander Hamilton, the first secretary of the treasury, and John Jay, the first chief justice of the Supreme Court, were both graduates of King's College. Presidents Theodore Roosevelt and Franklin Delano Roosevelt attended Columbia's Law School. Dwight Eisenhower served as president of Columbia University before becoming president of the United States.

Other famous Columbia alumni include Senator Barack Obama, former secretary of state Madeleine Albright, Supreme Court justice Ruth Bader Ginsburg, Broadway composer Richard Rodgers and his lyricists Lorenz Hart and Oscar Hammerstein II, singer Art Garfunkel, novelists Jack Kerouac, J. D. Salinger, and Upton Sinclair, science-fiction giant Isaac Asimov, poet Allen Ginsberg, and baseball player Lou Gehrig.

Anna Paquin and Famke Janssen, who played Rogue and Phoenix, respectively, in the *X-Men* movies, are both Columbia alumnae. Simon Kinberg, one of the screenwriters for *X-Men: The Last Stand* (2006), received an MFA from the film division of Columbia's School of the Arts.

It should not be remarkable that a number of Marvel characters are Columbia alumni as well.

Reed Richards of the Fantastic Four attended Columbia, as well as Harvard, Cal Tech, and "State University" in upstate New

York. While he was a graduate student at Columbia, Richards lived in a boardinghouse where he first met his landlady's niece, Susan Storm, who was then only twelve years old; years later Susan became Reed's wife.

Charles Xavier earned a doctorate in anthropology at Columbia before going on to receive a Ph.D. in genetics at Oxford. Many years later, after becoming a famous advocate of mutant rights, Xavier became a visiting professor in genetics at Columbia. One night Xavier was beaten nearly to death by a gang of Columbia students who hated mutants (*Uncanny X-Men* #192, April 1985).

Matt Murdock, the future Daredevil, met his best friend and future law partner, Franklin "Foggy" Nelson, when they were both students at the Columbia Law School. During this time Matt met and fell in love with a Columbia political-science student, Elektra Natchios, who cut short her studies when her father was killed. Daredevil met her again after she had become the costumed assassin Elektra (*Daredevil,* vol. 1, #168, January 1981). In the alternate continuity of Marvel's Ultimate line, Matt Murdock and Elektra were both undergraduates at Columbia.

Among the Marvel characters who have served as members of the Columbia faculty is Dr. James Power, a professor of physics who is also the father of the superpowered children known as Power Pack.

Lee Wing, a professor of Asian studies at Columbia, is the father of Colleen Wing, the friend and ally of the Super Hero Iron Fist. Colleen and Misty Knight, her partner in the detective firm Nightwing Restorations, are the martial artists known as the Daughters of the Dragon.

Another Columbia faculty member became the exorcist known as Gabriel the Devil-Hunter (*Monsters Unleashed* #11, April 1975).

When Tony Stark, the future Iron Man, was a teenager, his first girlfriend was Meredith McCall, who grew up to become a professor at Columbia.

In the 1940s Simon Meke, a criminal mastermind with the code name Isbisa, attempted to steal an atomic bomb as part of his plot to take over the world, but was foiled by the All-Winners Squad, a newly founded team of Super Heroes. Decades later, Isbisa became a professor of physics at Columbia University under the alias Dr. Sanderson (perhaps named after this book's author, a Columbia grad). Sanderson invented a device that could teleport people through time and space, and he and some of his students used it to pit various superpowered heroes and villains against the She-Hulk. Finally, the She-Hulk's friend Louise Mason, a former Super Heroine from the 1940s, recognized Sanderson as Isbisa. He fled, abandoning his assumed identity and his post at Columbia (*The Sensational She-Hulk* #29–30, July–August 1991).

New York City police officers Jeff Piper and Mike Badilino were assigned to investigate an incident at Columbia and discovered that the perpetrator was the Werewolf by Night, who fled, pursued by the Super Hero Moon Knight (*Code of Honor* #1, January 1997).

Columbia University also plays a prominent role in the *Spider-Man* movies.

In the first *Spider-Man* (2002) Peter Parker and Mary Jane Watson are on a high school field trip to Columbia's genetic research laboratory. There, Peter is bitten by a genetically altered spider, endowing him with the superpowers of Spider-Man. In the comics, on the other hand, Peter was visiting an atomic research laboratory, later identified as General Techtonics, and the spider was radioactive.

In *Spider-Man 2* (2004), Peter is a student at Columbia, presumably on a scholarship. One of his teachers there is Dr. Curt Connors, who presumably has not yet become Spider-Man's reptilian enemy, the Lizard, as he does in the comics. ✱

RIVERSIDE CHURCH
490 Riverside Drive

ONE OF NEW YORK City's leading places of worship, Riverside Church is an interdenominational Christian church. Built atop one of the highest points in the city, Riverside Church overlooks the Hudson River and is situated on the borders of Morningside Heights and Harlem.

Riverside Church was modeled after Chartres Cathedral, one of the most celebrated Gothic cathedrals in France, which was erected in the thirteenth century. Construction on Riverside Church began in 1927, and its first service was held three years later.

The church dominates the surrounding neighborhood, thanks to its remarkable tower, which is 392 feet tall. One of the tower's bells is the largest turned bell in the world, weighing twenty tons. The building takes up two city blocks, from West 120th to West 122nd Street, and from Riverside Drive to Claremont Avenue.

Among the noteworthy individuals who have spoken at Riverside Church are Dr. Martin Luther King Jr. and Nelson Mandela. Dr. William Sloane Coffin Jr., a celebrated activist against the Vietnam War, was senior minister at the church from 1977 to 1987.

Riverside Church is where John Jameson was to marry Mary Jane Watson at the end of the movie *Spider-Man 2* (2004). However, Mary Jane changes her mind at the last minute and runs from the church, down to Peter Parker's apartment to confess her love for him.

The exterior of Peter's apartment building was shot on the Lower East Side, so MJ must have been quite a marathon runner to get down there, still wearing her wedding gown! However, since in the movies Peter is a student at Columbia University, which is only a few blocks from Riverside Church, his apartment was presumably meant to be nearby.

In the comics John Jameson was never romantically involved with Mary Jane, and he ended up marrying, of all people, Jennifer Walters, the She-Hulk. ✳

RIVERSIDE CHURCH

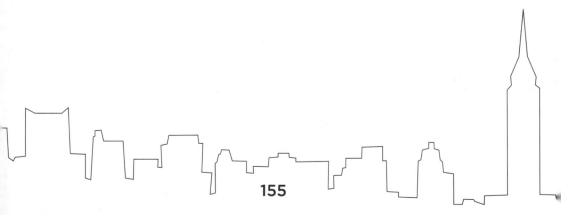

HARLEM

Upper Manhattan below Washington Heights, between the East and Hudson Rivers

HARLEM IS A FAMED section of upper Manhattan with a primarily African-American population. On the west side of Manhattan, Harlem begins at 125th Street, above Morningside Heights; Spanish Harlem, traditionally a Latino area, runs south of Morningside Heights down to 86th Street. Central Harlem, to the east of Morningside Heights, begins at 110th Street, along the north edge of Central Park. Harlem extends upward to 155th Street, where Washington Heights begins.

Harlem is probably best known for the cultural movement that bears its name, the Harlem Renaissance, in the 1920s.

Establishments such as the Cotton Club, the Apollo Theater, and the Savoy Ballroom were hotbeds of musical innovation and socialization, and a thriving theater scene was home to productions like Orson Welles's all-black staging of *Macbeth*.

Harlem is yet another section of Manhattan that has undergone a dramatic transformation and become more prosperous since the 1990s. (Former president Bill Clinton currently rents office space on West 125th Street.) However, for much of the twentieth century, Harlem, despite its rich cultural history, was one of the most economically depressed areas of the city.

In the Marvel Comics of the 1970s, Harlem was tyrannized by the powerful African-American crime lord known as Morgan, who debuted in *Captain America,* vol. 1, #152 (August 1972). He has long been opposed by two of Marvel's first African-American Super Heroes: the Falcon and Luke Cage, alias Power Man.

Sam Wilson, who became the Falcon, and Joe "Robbie" Robertson, who is now editor in chief of the *Daily Bugle,* both were born and grew up in Harlem. One of Robertson's high school classmates, Lonnie Lincoln, took a different turn in life and became the criminal known as Tombstone, an enemy of Spider-Man's.

As a small child, Ororo Munroe, who grew up to become Storm of the X-Men, also lived in Harlem with her parents. She revisited their apartment building in *Uncanny X-Men* #122 (June 1979), only to find it occupied by drug addicts.

Sam Wilson and Luke Cage (with his wife, former Super Hero Jessica Jones) currently make their homes in Harlem. And T'Challa, the Super Hero known as the Black Panther, once taught school there under the secret identity of Luke Charles.

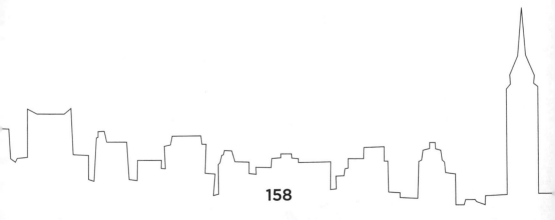

CITY COLLEGE
138th Street and Convent Avenue

THE CITY COLLEGE OF New York is the oldest division of the City University of New York, the largest urban public university in the United States. City College dates back to 1847, when it was known as the Free Academy. The latter name is apt, since until 1976 City College did not charge its students tuition. Even today, City College tuition for New York State residents remains quite low compared with that for private universities.

In 1906, City College moved to its current location, a thirty-five-acre campus, spanning from 131st to 141st Streets, on a hill overlooking Harlem. Many of the neo-Gothic buildings on campus are now considered architectural landmarks.

Famous alumni of City College include lyricist Ira Gershwin; former secretary of state Colin Powell; Mario Puzo, writer of *The Godfather;* actor Edward G. Robinson; Dr. Jonas Salk, discoverer of the polio vaccine; and novelist Upton Sinclair.

Years ago, the Eternals, a superhuman offshoot of humanity, decided to make their existence known to the rest of the human race. To this end, Margo Damian, a human friend of the Eternals', contacted her father's colleague Dr. Samuel Holden, a professor of anthropology at City College. Soon afterward, Dr. Holden introduced Ikaris, Sersi, Thena, and Makkari, all

Eternals, and Kro, a member of another racial offshoot, the Deviants, to his City College students (*The Eternals,* vol. 1, #6, December 1976). Dr. Holden continued to lecture about the Eternals, the Deviants, and their creators, the Celestials, at City College (*The Eternals,* vol. 2, #1, October 1985).

When the Fourth Host of the Celestials departed Earth, the human race lost their memories of these three races. However, Dr. Holden was allowed to retain his memories. Holden also retained another benefit of his contact with the Eternals: his long-standing relationship with the seductive Eternal Sersi.

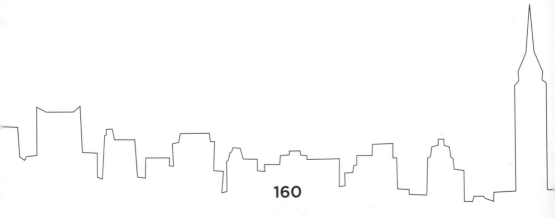

THE CLOISTERS
Fort Tryon Park

THE CLOISTERS IS A branch of the Metropolitan Museum of Art that is devoted to medieval European art. This satellite museum takes its name from the five actual medieval cloisters (quadrangles surrounded by roofed passageways) from European monasteries that were incorporated into the building's structure. The most famous pieces of art at the museum include the so-called Unicorn tapestries, from the Netherlands, and illuminated books such as the Limbourg brothers' Book of Hours.

John D. Rockefeller Jr. financed the Metropolitan Museum's acquisition of the original collection of medieval art for the

Cloisters. Rockefeller also paid for the creation of Fort Tryon Park, in which the Cloisters was erected, and purchased and then donated the land directly across the Hudson River to the state of New Jersey in order to preserve the pristine view from the museum. Hence, visitors to the Cloisters can imagine themselves transported back to medieval times, with no modern buildings within sight. The Cloisters' celebrated gardens complete the romantic atmosphere.

The isolation of the Cloisters from the rest of Manhattan made it a perfect location for a planned gangland assassination. Dominic Tyrone and Silvio Manfredi, alias Silvermane, had been partners in ascending into the upper ranks of the New York Maggia. On becoming a Maggia leader, Silvermane treacherously ordered a hit on Tyrone. But Tyrone survived and, years later, sought revenge on the Maggia as a costumed vigilante called the Rapier. Tyrone arranged a clandestine nighttime meeting with Silvermane at the Cloisters. There Tyrone attacked Silvermane, but was prevented from killing him by the intervention of Spider- Man (*Spectacular Spider-Man Annual* #2, 1980). Silvermane shot the Rapier in the back, but the Rapier still managed to escape, only to be assassinated later by another vigilante, Scourge.

NEW YORK UNDERGROUND

MANHATTAN IS AN ISLAND of skyscrapers, where millions of people live and work high above the ground. In Marvel's New York, the population extends far beneath the ground as well. Entire communities, even warring empires, exist beneath Manhattan's streets, of which most New Yorkers remain oblivious.

According to urban legend in the real world, alligators live in the New York sewers. The story went that people bought baby alligators as pets, then flushed them down toilets when they grew too big, and the reptiles grew to adult size in the sewers. In the Marvel Universe the urban legend became reality. After Loki, the Norse god of evil, had transformed him into a frog, Thor led the alligators of New York's sewers against the marauding rats of Central Park (*Thor* #364–65, February–March, 1986).

Within the sewers also lives a community of pale-skinned savages who behave like members of a prehistoric, primitive tribe. The costumed crime-fighter Daredevil once descended into their realm and engaged in hand-to-hand combat with the sewer people's king, a massive brute who bore a strange resemblance to the New York crime boss the Kingpin (*Daredevil*, vol. 1, #180, March 1982).

Another underground community is known as the Night

People of Zero Street. The original members were inmates in an insane asylum on Zero Street, a fictional location somewhere in New York City. One patient, Dr. Abner Doolittle, was a nuclear physicist, who was allowed to continue working on his experiments there. Dr. Doolittle invented a device that transported the asylum into another dimension. There he became known as Brother Wonderful, the ruler of the other inmates. Brother Wonderful transported his subjects to Earth to steal supplies; since the robberies took place after dark, the inmates became known as the Night People. Eventually Captain America sealed the portal linking the Night People's dimension to Earth (*Captain America and the Falcon* #201–3, September–November 1976).

The Night People later returned to Earth, and at least some of them founded a shantytown in caverns beneath Central Park. They called their new underground home Zerotown, and various homeless people who found their way there joined the community, as did the Super Hero Demolition-Man, nicknamed D-Man (*Captain America,* vol. 1, #410–11, December 1992–January 1993; *Captain America,* vol. 1, #418, August 1993).

The most notorious of New York's underground communities was the Morlocks, whom X-Men writer Chris Claremont named after the subterranean race in H. G. Wells's science-fiction novel *The Time Machine* (1895). Marvel's Morlock community first appeared in *Uncanny X-Men* #169 (May 1983). The Morlocks were mutants who had formed their own society beneath Manhattan's streets. Many of the Morlocks were outcasts in the aboveground world due to mutations that made them look physically grotesque. The Morlock known as Masque had the mutant ability to alter someone's physical appearance by touch and often used it to render normal-looking Morlocks hideous in order to fit in with the rest of the community.

The Morlocks inhabited a network of tunnels that the U.S. government constructed as fallout shelters during the Cold War period of the 1950s and then abandoned. This network not only runs under New York City but extends into New Jersey and Connecticut. The principal tunnel, known as the Alley, is fifty feet high and extends along the length of Manhattan Island.

The Morlocks were led

by a mutant woman named Callisto (who also appears in the 2006 movie *X-Men: The Last Stand*), until she was defeated by Storm of the X-Men in a trial by combat. Storm, as victor, became the rightful ruler of the Morlocks, but Storm allowed Callisto to continue to rule in her absence.

Mister Sinister, a Super Villain who specializes in genetic engineering, once dispatched the Marauders, a team of super-powered assassins, to wipe out the Morlock community. The X-Men attempted to halt this "mutant massacre," but the Marauders succeeded in exterminating the great majority of the Morlocks (in *Uncanny X-Men* #210–11, October–November 1986, and other mutant-related series during that time). Most of the Morlocks who survived this genocide drowned when an insane mutant, Mikhail Rasputin, who had taken over leadership of the Morlocks, flooded their tunnels. (He actually transported the Morlocks to another dimension, where he once again set himself up as ruler.) Eighty percent of the relatively small number of Morlocks left alive were transformed into normal-looking humans, lacking superpowers, by the events of the "House of M" story line (2005).

Nonetheless, to this day, a handful of Morlocks still live in the tunnels, currently under the leadership of Marrow, a former member of the X-Men.

Far, far beneath Manhattan's sewers and even the Morlocks'

tunnels lie the immense caverns that comprise the underground realm of Subterranea. These caverns are populated by various races of Subterraneans, humanoid creatures that were genetically engineered by the Deviants, an offshoot of the human race. The Deviants bred the two most populous races of Subterraneans to be subservient and incapable of complex, independent thought, so that they would serve their creators as slaves. However, the Deviants eventually abandoned the Subterraneans, who were left to fend for themselves in Subterranea for millennia.

A GALLERY OF THE FANTASTIC FOUR'S MOST FAMOUS FOES!

THE MOLE MAN

FROM F.F. # 1 NOV.

THE MOLE MAN! NEARLY BLIND INHABITANT OF THE NETHER REGIONS OF EARTH! USING HIS STRANGE "RADAR-SENSE" INSTEAD OF EYESIGHT, AIDED BY AN AWESOME GROUP OF UNDEREARTH MONSTERS, THIS BITTER, BROODING MAN YEARS AGO LEFT EARTH'S SURFACE BECAUSE OF HIS HATRED FOR MANKIND, AND SET UP AN UNDERGROUND EMPIRE OVER WHICH HE RULED WITH TYRANNICAL POWER... UNTIL THE FANTASTIC FOUR PUT AN END TO HIS SAVAGE DREAM OF CONQUERING THE SURFACE OF EARTH!

Then, the wizard Merlin banished the last emperor of Rome, known as Tyrannus, to Subterranea, where Tyrannus not only discovered a "fountain of youth" that has extended his life, but also became the master of the orange-skinned race of Subterraneans, whom he renamed the Tyrannoids.

In modern times, another surface dweller found his way to Subterranea and dubbed himself the Mole Man. He became the ruler of the yellow-skinned race of Subterraneans, called the Moloids.

For years now, when they are not fighting wars against each other, the Mole Man and Tyrannus have each repeatedly sought to invade and conquer the surface world. New York City apparently lies above a crossroads between their respective empires, since each of them has attacked the city. The Mole Man's first invasion of Manhattan took place in *Fantastic Four,* vol. 1, #31 (October 1964), while Tyrannus attacked New York in *Nova,* vol. 1, #5 (January 1977).

Two other races of Subterraneans are more intelligent and strong-willed than the Tyrannoids and Moloids. Grotesk, the last of the Gortokian Subterraneans, surfaced in the New York area and attempted in vain to destroy the world in *X-Men* (first series) #41–42 (February–March 1968). The other Subterranean race are called the Lava Men. One of the Lava Men, Molto, emerged in Manhattan and battled Thor in *Journey into Mystery* #97 (October 1963).

Of course millions of New Yorkers in the real world descend beneath its streets every day to ride the subways. Super Heroes rarely venture into the New York subway system, preferring to travel through the sky, like the web-slinging Spider-Man. The most prominent part that the New York subway system has played in Marvel history actually occurs aboveground. In some areas of the city, particularly in the outer boroughs, the subway trains emerge from underground and become elevated trains, riding on tracks high above the street. In the movie *Spider-Man 2* (2004), in a spectacular action sequence, Spider-Man battles Doctor Octopus on an onrushing R train high above the street and narrowly prevents it from plunging off the end of the tracks. ✱

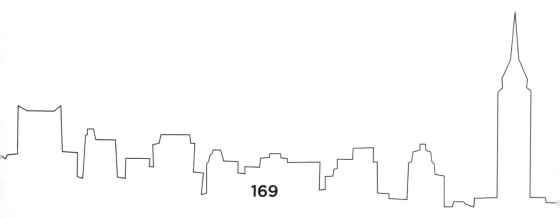

BROOKLYN BRIDGE, GEORGE WASHINGTON BRIDGE, QUEENSBORO BRIDGE, ROOSEVELT ISLAND

ONE OF THE MOST shocking events in the history of Marvel Comics is also the source of one of continuity's most nagging conundrums. In *Amazing Spider-Man* #121 (June 1973) the Green Goblin, who had discovered Spider-Man's secret identity, kidnapped Peter Parker's first true love, Gwen Stacy. The Goblin flew her to the top of a bridge, then hurled her toward the water below. Spider-Man swooped down on his webbing and managed to catch Gwen, but the shock of the impact still broke her neck: she was dead.

But which bridge witnessed this dramatic scene? According to writer Gerry Conway's text, it was the George Washington Bridge, which connects northern Manhattan to New Jersey across the Hudson River. But artist Gil Kane drew the Brooklyn Bridge, which connects lower Manhattan to Brooklyn across the East River!

Since comics is a medium of visual storytelling, Kane gets the edge. The retelling of the story of Gwen's death in *Marvels* #4 (April 1994), illustrated by Alex Ross, clearly shows the Brooklyn Bridge.

The first *Spider-Man* movie (2002) devised a variation on the scene of Gwen's demise. This time it was Mary Jane Watson whom the Green Goblin dropped from atop a bridge. But this was yet a third bridge. Amping up the tension, in the movie the Goblin also sent a Roosevelt Island tram plummeting to its doom, in an attempt to force Spider-Man to choose between saving the woman he loved or rescuing all the passengers. This had a happier ending than *Amazing Spider-Man* #121: Spider-Man managed to save everyone. The one exception was the Goblin himself, who died moments later in battle with Spider-Man in a deserted area of Roosevelt Island.

Named after President Franklin D. Roosevelt, Roosevelt Island lies in the East River between Manhattan and Queens. The island is primarily a residential area, with many apartment dwellers, but there are only a few means of getting back and forth. The Roosevelt Island Bridge connects the island to Queens, and a subway station opened in 1989. Before then, the only direct way to travel from Manhattan to Roosevelt Island was by the aerial tramway, which opened in 1976. Each car holds 125 passengers.

Roosevelt Island is situated beneath the Queensboro Bridge, which is also known as the Fifty-ninth Street Bridge. Opened to the public in 1909, this bridge connects Manhattan to the borough of Queens. So the bridge in the movie, since it runs alongside the Roosevelt Island tramway, must be the Queensboro Bridge.

The Brooklyn Bridge, easily the most recognizable of New York City's bridges, was opened in 1883 and, at that time, was the world's longest suspension bridge. It is 5,989 feet long. The George Washington Bridge opened in 1931 and is somewhat shorter, running 4,760 feet long. All three of these bridges have seen their share of action in the Marvel Universe.

At the climax of their battle with the flying monster called the Griffin, Spider-Man and the Beast knocked him out of the sky onto the Brooklyn Bridge (*Marvel Team-Up,* vol. 1, #38, October 1975).

Seeking vengeance on Spider-Man and newspaper publisher J. Jonah Jameson, another criminal scientist, Spencer Smythe, caused Jameson's son John to fall from atop the Brooklyn Bridge (*Amazing Spider-Man* #190, March 1979), but John was teleported to safety.

Captain America first encountered and fought the Native American superhuman called the Black Crow atop the Brooklyn Bridge (*Captain America* #292, April 1984).

Contemplating suicide, former criminal inventor Fabian Stankowitz climbed to the top of the Brooklyn Bridge. A vigilante called Blistik tried to force Stankowitz to jump, but Captain America hurled his shield at Blistik, who fell into the East River himself (*Captain America* #422, December 1993).

Another would-be suicide, Spider-Man's longtime foe the Chameleon, did actually jump off the Brooklyn Bridge (*Webspinners: Tales of Spider-Man* #11, December 1999), but somehow survived.

After the death of Gwen Stacy, Peter Parker fell in love with Mary Jane Watson. So the original Green Goblin, years later, captured Mary Jane and this time threw her off the George Washington Bridge. Learning from his mistakes, Spider-Man successfully rescued MJ. Another Spider-Man archfoe, Doctor Octopus, abruptly turned up, battled the Goblin atop the bridge, and both fell into the Hudson River (*Marvel Knights: Spider-Man* #11, April 2005).

A superhuman murderer named Francis Klum once abducted the Black Cat and brought her to the top of the Queensboro Bridge (*Spider-Man and Black Cat: The Evil That Men Do* #5, February 2006).

In an alternate future, Peter Parker and Mary Jane have a teenage daughter named May. When the middle-aged Parker accepted a challenge by a new Green Goblin to fight him at the Brooklyn Bridge, the superpowered May battled the Goblin and saved her father's life, thus inaugurating her career as Spider-Girl (*What If?*, vol. 2, #105, February 1998).

In another alternate reality depicted in Marvel's Ultimate line of comics, the Green Goblin hurled Mary Jane Watson from the top of the Queensboro Bridge, but the Ultimate Spider-Man saved her life (*Ultimate Spider-Man* #25, October 2002). In the Ultimate reality, Magneto and his terrorist mutant Brotherhood destroyed the Brooklyn Bridge, killing hundreds of innocent people (*Ultimate War* #1, January 2003).

The Brooklyn Bridge has repeatedly been destroyed and rebuilt in the "mainstream" Marvel timeline as well. A monster commanded by Dragonrider, a member of the Atlantean strike force Fathom Five, demolished the Brooklyn Bridge in their attack on New York City (*New Thunderbolts* #4, April 2005). Years earlier, the criminal organization Zodiac wrecked all of the bridges leading into Manhattan when they took the whole island hostage (*Avengers* #82, November 1970). Obviously, the bridges were all reconstructed in remarkably short time to appear in all these other stories.

The Brooklyn Bridge is also a site of a famous sequence in the first *Fantastic Four* movie (2005), although the bridge itself was computer-generated. ✻

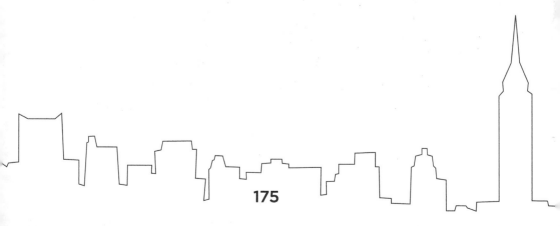

ELLIS ISLAND
New York Harbor

FROM 1892 TO 1954, millions of immigrants from Europe set foot in the United States for the first time when they arrived on Ellis Island, one of the principal stations for processing immigrants who arrived by sea. Today it is the site of a museum commemorating the island's role in the great waves of immigration in the first half of the twentieth century.

The original island is a part of New York City. However, additional sections of the island, created through landfill deposits, are legally part of the state of New Jersey. This, however, is ultimately a moot point since the island is owned by the federal government and is part of the Statue of Liberty National Monument. (The statue stands on nearby Liberty Island.)

Ellis Island's most prominent role in Marvel history is in the first *X-Men* movie (2000). The United Nations holds a special conference on Ellis Island to discuss, among other issues, the rising number of mutants in the world. The mutant terrorist leader Magneto schemes to use a device he has installed at the Statue of Liberty to irradiate the dignitaries attending the conference, transforming them into mutants. In the movie's final act, while the conference opens on Ellis Island, the X-Men battle and defeat Magneto and his allies in and atop the statue nearby.

Ellis Island's symbolism makes it a target. Hence, Spider-Man once thwarted an attempt to destroy the island by soldiers from ULTIMATUM, a terrorist organization opposed to all national governments (*Amazing Spider-Man,* vol. 1, #324, November 1989).

It was on Ellis Island that criminal scientist Simon Marshall experimented on teenage runaways to develop a new addictive narcotic drug. By injecting his experimental drug into two unsuspecting victims, Tyrone Johnson and Tandy Bowen, he triggered their transformations into the superpowered vigilantes Cloak and Dagger (*Spectacular Spider-Man* #64, March 1982).

The Native American mutant Charles Little Sky, also known as Portal, once got a job at Ellis Island. There he encountered three Avengers who were visiting the island: Captain America, Thor, and the legendary hero Gilgamesh, a member of the race of Eternals. When another superpowered Native American, the Puma, unexpectedly showed up to take Little Sky back to his tribe, the Avengers leapt to Portal's defense. Portal then opened an interdimensional gateway, through which a team of Super Villains, the U-Foes, arrived. While the Avengers and

Puma battled the U-Foes on Ellis Island, Portal made his escape (*Avengers,* vol. 1, #304, June 1989).

Also, Spider-Man once met on Ellis Island with the mercenary Silver Sable and three members of the team called the Outlaws, the Prowler, the Rocket Racer, and the Sandman (*Web of Spider-Man* #50, May 1989), to defend himself against allegations made in the *Daily Bugle* that Spider-Man had turned to a life of crime.

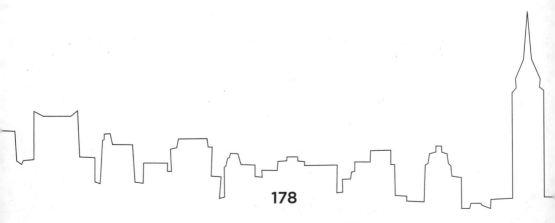

RIKERS ISLAND/RYKER'S ISLAND
East River

NEW YORK'S LARGEST PRISON and the island on which it stands are known as Rikers Island. But in the Marvel Universe the fictionalized versions of the prison and island are called Ryker's Island. Marvel's version is actually closer to the name of the man for whom the island was named—Abraham Rycken, a Dutchman who settled on Long Island in 1638 and whose descendants originally owned Rikers Island.

Rikers/Ryker's Island lies in the East River between the Bronx and Queens, just offshore from LaGuardia Airport. In the real world, Rikers Island prison holds around fifteen thousand inmates. However, none of them are long-term prisoners: they are either awaiting trial or serving sentences of one year or less. Hence, except for temporary transfers from other prisons, Rikers inmates generally do not include the worst of the hard-core criminals.

Matters are very different in the Marvel Universe, since its version of New York City has more Super Villains per capita than anywhere else on Earth. Marvel's Ryker's is populated by not only conventional criminals but also superhuman prisoners who are serving long-term sentences.

Marvel's version first appeared in *Amazing Spider-Man* #4

(September 1963) as part of the origin story for the villain Sandman, although it was not named Ryker's until many years later. Famous Ryker's Island inmates include the Punisher, Bullseye, and Kingpin.

In the 1980s, the U.S. government built the Vault, a maximum-security prison specifically designed to incarcerate superpowered criminals, located far from New York City. Supposedly escape-proof, the Vault was nevertheless the site of repeated prison breaks and was finally destroyed.

Rather than continue to place all the bad eggs in a single basket, the federal government then decided to imprison Super Villains at various maximum-security facilities around the country. One of these is the Raft, a specially designed maximum-security prison considered an offshoot of Ryker's, on an island near Ryker's Island, which first appeared in *Alias* #26 (November 2003). Not only are the cells beneath water level, but they are made of steel and lined with unbreakable adamantium. Special devices neutralize the inmates' superpowers.

Despite all of these precautions, there was recently a major prison break in which forty-two prisoners escaped from the Raft (*New Avengers* #1, January 2005). Nonetheless, the Raft remains in operation. ✷

STATUE OF LIBERTY

Liberty Island, New York Harbor

LIBERTY ENLIGHTENING the World is the true name of the Statue of Liberty, a gift from France to the United States of America. As its title indicates, the colossal statue depicts the allegorical figure of Liberty as a crowned, robed woman, raising a flaming torch, while holding a tablet marked with the date of the Declaration of Independence. The French sculptor Frédéric-Auguste Bartholdi designed the statue, which stands 151 feet and one inch tall atop a base that is 154 feet high. Although the statue was originally intended to commemorate America's centennial, it was not finished until years later. President Grover Cleveland dedicated the Statue of Liberty on October 28, 1886.

For years visitors were allowed to go inside the statue, and even to peer out from its torch and crown. However, following the September 11, 2001, attack on the World Trade Center, the statue is no longer open to the public. Visitors may still travel by ferry from lower Manhattan to Liberty Island, where the statue stands, and visit the museum housed in the statue's base.

The symbolism of the Statue of Liberty has made it a tempting target for terrorists and Super Villains through over sixty years of Marvel history.

In January 1945 the Super Hero known as the Blazing Skull thwarted a plot by Nazi saboteurs, led by the Masked Raider, to blow up the Statue of Liberty (*Midnight Sons Unlimited* #9, May 1995).

Sometime between World War II and the origin of the Fantastic Four, the gargantuan creature called Gorgilla invaded New York City, and a team called the Monster Hunters pursued him out to the Statue of Liberty, where they subdued the manlike beast (*Marvel Universe* #5, October 1998).

For many years, beginning in *Strange Tales Annual* #2 (1963), Spider-Man and the Human Torch have used the top of the Statue of Liberty as their private meeting place. The

Torch can easily fly there, but presumably Spider-Man has to get out there by boat and then use his webbing to swing up to the top.

In an attempt to conquer the United States, the Asian mastermind called the Yellow Claw dispatched troops to Liberty Island. There they were to activate the Claw's "id paralyzer," which would turn the people of America into his slaves. Using weaponry created by Mr. Fantastic, Captain America and SHIELD director Nick Fury foiled the Yellow Claw's scheme (*Strange Tales,* vol. 1, #160–61, September–October 1967).

Daredevil's spectacular battle against his costumed adversary the Jester atop the Statue of Liberty was featured on the cover of *Daredevil,* vol. 1, #45 (October 1968).

Burt Worthington, the uncle of the Angel, a member of the X-Men, is also the costumed criminal who called himself the Dazzler. (This Dazzler should not be confused with the later mutant disco singer of the same name.) Plotting to conquer the world, Worthington demonstrated his sense of irony by establishing his secret base beneath the Statue of Liberty, somehow building it without being detected by the Liberty Island guards (*Ka-Zar* #2–3, December 1970–March 1971; *Marvel Tales* #30, April 1971).

On one of his numerous rampages through New York City, the Incredible Hulk took refuge atop the Statue of Liberty. Surprisingly, a wealthy young feminist named Samantha Parrington persuaded the Hulk to descend from the statue peacefully (*Incredible Hulk* #142, August 1971). Parrington was subsequently transformed into a superpowered double for the Asgardian goddess Brunnhilde, the Valkyrie.

As the site of so many violent episodes in Marvel history, the Statue of Liberty could not forever escape being seriously damaged. The Plunderer, the costumed nemesis of his brother, Ka-Zar, lord of the Savage Land, gained control over yet another gigantic creature, the extraterrestrial called Gog. During a battle in New York City, Gog seized Ka-Zar and took him and the Plunderer to Liberty Island. Gog then climbed up the Statue of Liberty and tore off the hand carrying its torch. From there Gog teleported himself to the top of one of the World Trade Center towers, and from there teleported again, disappearing from New York City (*Astonishing Tales* #18,

June 1973). The city's Super Heroes subsequently repaired the Statue of Liberty, restoring its severed hand and torch.

A terrorist organization called the People's Liberation Front hired a costumed assassin named the Hitman to abduct *Daily Bugle* publisher J. Jonah Jameson. The Hitman took Jameson to the Statue of Liberty, which the PLF intended to blow up with Jameson inside. Spider-Man and the Punisher arrived at Liberty Island and overpowered the PLF forces, and the Hitman shot the terrorist leader dead before he could blow up the statue with everyone still inside. Still holding Jameson hostage, the Hitman shot Spider-Man in the arm, causing him to fall from the statue's crown. As the Punisher confronted the Hitman atop the crown, Spider-Man returned, grabbed Jameson, and the Punisher shot the Hitman. Spider-Man, Jameson, and the Hitman all ended up precariously holding on to the statue's crown. The Punisher rescued Jameson and Spider-Man, but allowed the Hitman to fall to his death (*Amazing Spider-Man*, vol. 1, #175, December 1977).

As mentioned elsewhere in this book, the jaded members of the Gotham Game Club once set themselves the challenge of destroying the Hulk when he next appeared in New York City. Club member and shipping magnate James Logan attacked the Hulk from a helicopter, driving him out into New York Harbor near Liberty Island. Then Logan fired cannons at the

STATUE OF LIBERTY

Hulk from the ocean liner *Ocean Queen*. The Hulk responded by sinking the immense boat! (*Incredible Hulk Annual* #9, 1980.)

A costumed fanatic who called himself the Everyman threatened to kill innocent people unless Captain America fought a duel with him at the Statue of Liberty. The Captain accepted the challenge and overpowered Everyman (*Captain America*, vol. 1, #267, March 1982).

Kofi, a member of the alien Kymellian race, traveled to Earth by starship to warn Power Pack, a team of child Super Heroes, that they were in danger. Kofi's ship was shot down near the Statue of Liberty, but he survived, though injured (*Power Pack* #16, November 1985).

During the demonic invasion of New York in the "Inferno" story line, the Statue of Liberty, animated by demons, began snarling at tourists (*Amazing Spider-Man*, vol. 1, #312, February 1989). Once the demons were gone, the statue returned to its usual—apparent—lifelessness.

The Griffin, a human criminal who was transformed into a winged creature resembling a lion, once abducted the Sub-Mariner's friend Carrie Alexander and flew with her to the Statue of Liberty. The Sub-Mariner pursued them there and battled the Griffin at the statue (*Namor the Sub-Mariner* #2, May 1990).

Another terrorist, the Irish mutant Leila O'Toole, alias Plasma, launched an attack on the Statue of Liberty that was thwarted by Moon Knight and Ghost Rider (*Moon Knight,* vol. 3, #25, April 1991).

You would think that it would be impossible to steal something as immense as the Statue of Liberty, but you would be wrong. A Japanese female master criminal code-named Cathode succeeded, using a shrinking ray to reduce the statue to a size she could transport. The U.S. government hired the mercenary Silver Sable and her Wild Pack to get it back (*Silver Sable and the Wild Pack* #6–7, November–December 1992).

After the statue was restored to its rightful size and place, the murderous villains Carnage and Shriek tortured the superhuman Venom within its torch during the "Maximum Carnage" story line (*Web of Spider-Man* #103, August 1993).

Afterward, the statue became the target of Psiphon, still

another terrorist leader, with mutant powers. Psiphon and his men captured innocent people at the Statue of Liberty and suspended them from the statue's crown. Psiphon demanded $50 million for the hostages' release. Michael Badilino, who was the superhuman vigilante Vengeance, killed the other terrorists and literally kicked Psiphon off the top of the statue. Psiphon's mutant powers enabled him to survive the fall, but he was taken into police custody (*Marvel Comics Presents* #148, February 1994).

The team of former Super Villains called the Thunderbolts battled and defeated the superstrong Wrecking Crew at the Statue of Liberty (*Thunderbolts* #1, April 1997).

In the most recent attempt to blow up the Statue of Liberty, the Grim Reaper trapped the members of Heroes for Hire in a ship containing a bomb, intending them to die in the explosion. Both the statue and the Super Heroes survived (*Heroes for Hire* #7, 2007).

On a parallel Earth in an alternate timeline, the cyborg Deathlok battled and defeated another cyborg, War-Wolf, atop the base of the Statue of Liberty (*Astonishing Tales* #26–27, October–December 1974). The freedom fighter Godwulf, who has been both Deathlok's ally and enemy, had his base at the statue.

In the alternate continuity of Marvel's Ultimate line of books, the Statue of Liberty was pulled down and destroyed (*Ultimates* #9, vol. 2, December 2005).

In the *Spider-Man 2* video game, Mysterio transforms the Statue of Liberty into a statue of himself, and Spider-Man has to change it back by destroying Mysterio's power core.

In the climactic sequence of the first *X-Men* movie (2000), the mutant Magneto installed at the top of the Statue of Liberty a machine that can artificially mutate ordinary human beings. Having captured the young mutant Rogue, Magneto planned to temporarily transfer his magnetic powers to her and use her to power the mutation machine, a process that would kill her. A summit of world leaders was being held nearby on Ellis Island; Magneto planned to use the machine to forcibly transform them all into mutants. The X-Men battled Magneto's Brotherhood in the Liberty Island museum and atop the statue itself, rescuing Rogue and destroying Magneto's machine.

The Statue of Liberty's most startling appearance in Marvel history came in *Amazing Adult Fantasy* #13 (June 1962), shortly before the debut of Spider-Man in issue 15. The Undersea Giants were a race of amphibious creatures that were twenty feet tall and dwelled in the ocean depths. Fearing they would be discovered by humans, the Giants launched a preemptive attack on New York City one night. However, the Giants were thrust back into the ocean by a mysterious assailant whose size dwarfed their own.

The next day repairmen were sent to the Statue of Liberty because the knuckles of its right hand had mysteriously been damaged overnight.

Could it be that the Statue of Liberty is alive? That it is the goddess of Liberty herself standing guard at the traditional entryway to America? We may never know for sure. ✳

THE BRONX

EACH OF NEW YORK City's boroughs is located on an island except for its northernmost borough, the Bronx.

Despite its pastoral heritage—part of the borough started out as "Bronck's farm"—the Bronx is a dense urban area that went into a particularly sharp decline in the 1960s and 1970s. The South Bronx especially became notorious as a dangerous area. Wilson Fisk, the Kingpin of Crime, started out as a small-time criminal in the Bronx (*Flashback: Amazing Spider-Man*, July 1997). In the Marvel Universe, the South Bronx was guarded by the Wolfpack, a team of teenage crime-fighters (*Marvel Graphic Novel* #31: *Wolfpack,* 1987). The criminal organization called the Serpent Society had its first headquarters in the South Bronx. Much of the South Bronx was destroyed in a tremendous battle between Thor and the alien warrior woman Stellaris (*Thor,* vol. 1, #419–20, July–August 1990).

Apart from Yankee Stadium, the Bronx's most famous tourist attraction is the Bronx Zoo, formerly known as the New York Zoological Park. Covering 265 acres and holding over four hundred species of animals, including lions, tigers, elephants, gorillas, and bears, it is the largest metropolitan zoo in the United States.

A man-size, humanoid reptile called the Iguana first encountered Spider-Man at the Bronx Zoo's Reptile House

THE BRONX

(*Spectacular Spider-Man,* vol. 1, #32, July 1979). A villain called the Man-Elephant transformed the elephants at the Bronx Zoo into half-human, half-pachyderm creatures, only to be trampled by them when they panicked (*The Sensational She-Hulk* #51, May 1993).

According to her origin story, zoologist Shanna O'Hara worked with leopards at the Central Park Zoo before moving to Africa, where she became

the adventuress Shanna the She-Devil (*Shanna the She-Devil,* vol. 1, #1, December 1972). Since there have been no leopards or other large members of the cat family at the Central Park Zoo for decades, it is now more likely that Shanna was employed at the Bronx Zoo.

In the alternate future time known as the Days of Future Past, mutants, including members of the X-Men, are imprisoned in a concentration camp known as the South Bronx Mutant Containment Facility (*Uncanny X-Men* #141–42, January–February 1981). ✷

YANKEE STADIUM
East 161st Street and River Avenue, the Bronx

ONE OF THE MOST famous sports facilities in the United States, Yankee Stadium has been home to baseball's New York Yankees since it opened in 1923. It is nicknamed the House That Ruth Built after the legendary baseball player Babe Ruth, a member of the Yankees. Yankee Stadium was the home of football's New York Giants from 1956 to 1973 and was a prominent venue for professional boxing as well.

With sixty thousand seats, Yankee Stadium was twice as big as the typical ballpark at the time it first opened. Indeed, due to its size, Yankee Stadium was the first baseball facility that was actually called a stadium.

That sheer size makes Yankee Stadium the perfect setting for another sort of "sport" in the Marvel Universe: hunting monsters.

In the late 1950s, Ulysses Bloodstone and other adventurers formed a team called the Monster Hunters to combat and capture the gigantic monsters that were turning up around the world. After being transported to New York City, the gargantuan apelike creature Gorgilla went on a rampage at Yankee Stadium. The Monster Hunters quickly showed up and attempted to subdue him. Gorgilla escaped and made his way to the Statue of Liberty, where one of the Monster Hunters, Doctor Druid, finally succeeded in calming the colossal man-beast, and the Monster Hunters tried to help him return to his home in Borneo (*Marvel Universe* #5, October 1998).

Rex Randolph was a worker for Damage Control, the construction unit that specializes in repairing damage caused by the battles of superhuman beings in New York City. After being exposed to a mysterious glowing sphere, Rex gained cosmic powers and flew off into outer space. On his return, months later, he called himself Edifice Rex, a super being dedicated to establishing "a world of perpetual neatness." His first act on Earth was to prevent a battle involving the Hulk, the New Warriors, and other Damage Control employees that was about to commence in Yankee Stadium (*Damage Control,* vol. 3, #2, July 1991).

The Yankees began construction on a new stadium, next to the original Yankee Stadium, in 2006. When the new Yankee Stadium is completed in 2009, the original stadium will be torn down. Whether any monsters will choose the new stadium as a venue for their rampages remains to be seen. ✳

BROOKLYN

THE BOROUGH OF BROOKLYN was actually a separate city until it was incorporated into New York City in 1898. Were Brooklyn still an independent city, it would be the third largest in the United States.

One of the most famous locations in Brooklyn is Coney Island, which is actually a peninsula on its southern coast. Starting in the mid-nineteenth century, New Yorkers flocked to the beach at Coney Island to escape the summer heat. Major amusement parks were built there, but the area went into decline following World War II. The Astroland amusement park remained, however, and its crown jewel is the Cyclone, one of the most famous roller coasters in the world.

BROOKLYN

Galactus, the gigantic "Devourer of Worlds," wrecked a Coney Island amusement park, presumably Astroland, while battling the Silver Surfer and the Fantastic Four in *Fantastic Four,* vol. 1, #122 (May 1972).

Daredevil and Bullseye once fought on the Cyclone roller coaster as Daredevil tried to rescue Black Widow from his foe (*Daredevil,* vol. 1, #161, November 1979).

In the real world there are currently plans to develop hotels and a new amusement park on the Astroland site.

In his secret identity of Steve Rogers, Captain America once lived in an apartment house at 569 Leaman Place in Brooklyn Heights. Later, Rogers owned a Brooklyn Heights costume shop that served as the front for the headquarters of his Hotline, a telephone and online service enabling people to contact him for help.

The thunder god Thor lived in another section of Brooklyn, Bay Ridge, under his mortal identity of construction worker Sigurd Jarlson.

After leaving their Manhattan bases, the young Super Hero team known as the New Warriors took over a former firehouse in the Brooklyn neighborhood known as DUMBO (Down Under Manhattan Bridge Overpass).

In the 1980s Marvel introduced a line of comics that were

set in an alternate reality called the New Universe. In the New York City of this continuity, Brooklyn had its own costumed Super Hero, who was named, of course, Captain Brooklyn, and debuted in *Justice* #31 (May 1989). There was also a Captain Manhattan, who first appeared in *D. P. 7* #30 (April 1989), but whether there was a Captain Bronx, a Captain Queens, or a Captain Staten Island remains a mystery. ✳

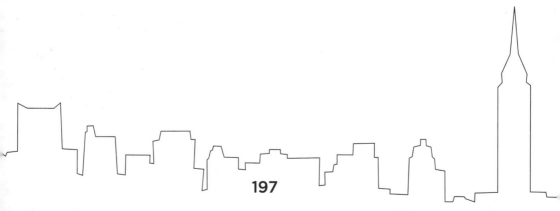

QUEENS

QUEENS, NEW YORK CITY'S largest borough, was named after Queen Catherine, the wife of England's seventeenth-century monarch King Charles II. Nearly half of Queens' population are immigrants, and more different ethnic groups live in Queens County than can be found in any other county in the United States. Shea Stadium is located in Queens, as are the city's two major airports, LaGuardia Airport and John F. Kennedy International Airport.

Many of Marvel's characters were born in Queens, including Peter Parker, alias Spider-Man, and Richard Rider, the Super Hero known as Nova.

Among Queens' various neighborhoods are Forest Hills, where Peter Parker was raised by his aunt May and uncle Ben, and Astoria, the location of Stark Industries facilities.

The Brand Corporation, a research and development firm that was owned by Roxxon Oil, had facilities in the section of Queens known as Jamaica, as well as on Long Island. As part of Roxxon's illegal covert activities, Brand secretly developed means of interdimensional transportation and endowed operatives with superhuman powers. The Avengers once invaded Brand's Queens plant, where they battled the Squadron Supreme, a Super Hero team from another Earth (*Avengers,* vol. 1, #141–49, November 1975–July 1976). ✳

FOREST HILLS
Queens

FOREST HILLS IS A middle-to-upper-class residential area of the borough of Queens. Although the area was first settled in the eighteenth century, the modern neighborhood of Forest Hills was founded in 1906. In the real world, Forest Hills may be best known as the former site of the U.S. Open tennis championship. In the Marvel Universe, however, Forest Hills' main importance is that it is where Peter Parker, the amazing Spider-Man, was raised by his aunt May and uncle Ben after his parents' deaths.

Next door to the Parkers lived Aunt May's best friend, Anna Watson, whose niece Mary Jane grew up to become Peter's girlfriend. In the first *Spider-Man* movie, Mary Jane lives in that house with her father, instead.

Forest Hills has a large middle-class population, many of whom are senior citizens, so it makes sense that May and Ben Parker and Anna Watson would have homes there.

Forest Hills' wealthier residents live in the large homes in the beautiful section known as Forest Hills Gardens. Designed by architect Grosvenor Atterbury, Forest Hills Gardens resembles an English village with its many beautiful houses in the Tudor style, complete with towers and spires. Frederick Law

Olmsted Jr., the son of one of the designers of Central Park, was the landscape architect for Forest Hills Gardens. Presumably this is where Peter Parker's wealthy classmate Liz Allan lived in their high school days.

Peter, Liz, and their classmate "Flash" Thompson all attended their local public high school. Presumably it was based on the actual Forest Hills High School, but writer Stan Lee dubbed the school Midtown High, an odd name, considering that New Yorkers generally apply the term *midtown* to Manhattan, not to the other boroughs. Midtown High made its debut on the first page of the very first Spider-Man story (*Amazing Fantasy* #15, 1962).

Jessica Jones, who later became a Super Heroine and the star of the comic book *Alias,* was another of Peter's classmates at Midtown High.

In the alternate continuity of the *Ultimate Spider-Man* series, Mary Jane also attends Midtown High. Peter, Mary Jane, and Flash all attend the same high school in the first *Spider-Man* movie (2002), but the name Midtown High is not used.

In the comics, the adult Peter Parker ended up getting a job as a science teacher at Midtown High, beginning in *Amazing Spider-Man,* vol. 2, #31 (July 2001). Flash Thompson currently works there as an athletic coach.

In *Amazing Spider-Man* #317 (July 1989), it was revealed that the Parkers lived at 20 Ingram Street in Forest Hills Gardens. However, the house used in the *Spider-Man* movies is on Sixty-ninth Road between Metropolitan Avenue and Sybilla Street.

Famous real-life residents of Forest Hills, past and present, include singers Paul Simon and Art Garfunkel, comedians Lou Costello, Ray Romano, and Jerry Seinfeld, composer Burt Bacharach, fashion designer Donna Karan, actor Carroll O'Connor (who played Queens resident Archie Bunker on *All in the Family*), and TV host Jerry Springer. ✻

JAMAICA BAY
Gateway National Recreation Area, Brooklyn and Queens

ONE OF THE MORE dramatic and significant events in Marvel history took place in *X-Men* (first series) #101 in Jamaica Bay, off the southwestern end of Long Island. Following a battle with Sentinel robots aboard a space station, the X-Men took a space shuttle back toward Earth. To get there, the shuttle had to travel through a solar radiation storm. As pilot, Jean Grey, one of the original X-Men, had to steer the craft from a section of the shuttle that lacked shielding sufficient to protect her from the intense radiation. The spacecraft crash-landed into Jamaica Bay, and the X-Men swam free of the shuttle. Then, to their amazement, they saw Jean rise from the waters into the sky, declaring that she had been transformed into the Phoenix.

Years later it would be revealed that a sentient cosmic power known as the Phoenix Force had duplicated Jean's body and taken on part of her consciousness. It was this being who joined the X-Men as Phoenix, went mad during the "Dark Phoenix Saga" (*Uncanny X-Men* #129–38, January–October 1980), which was the basis for the movie *X-Men: The Last Stand* (2006), and finally committed suicide. Upon the demise of this Phoenix, its borrowed portion of Jean's psyche returned to the real Jean Grey.

But where was she? The Phoenix Force had placed the real Jean into a comatose state within a strange cocoon that lay at the bottom of Jamaica Bay. Within that cocoon, Jean recovered from the damage the radiation had wreaked on her body. In *Avengers* #263 (January 1986), the Avengers discovered the cocoon, and Jean emerged from it in *Fantastic Four* #286

(January 1986). She has since adopted the name Phoenix.

Jamaica Bay must be considerably deeper in the Marvel Universe than in our world, since in the real New York it is a lagoon with an average depth of only thirteen feet!

The bay lies offshore from John F. Kennedy International Airport in Queens, one of the three major airports in the New York City

JAMAICA BAY

area. (The others are LaGuardia Airport, in northern Queens, and Newark Airport, in New Jersey.)

Jamaica Bay and its marshlands are an important habitat for local species of birds, fish, insects, and plant life. Hence the area is now the Jamaica Bay Wildlife Refuge, which is part of the Gateway National Recreation Area, run by the National Park Service. *

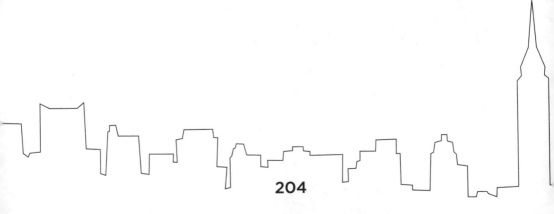

SHEA STADIUM
123-01 Roosevelt Avenue, Flushing, Queens

WILLIAM A. SHEA MUNICIPAL Stadium, which opened in 1964, is the longtime home of the baseball team the New York Mets. The football team, the New York Jets, also played at Shea Stadium from 1964 to 1983. Shea Stadium has also at times been a venue for rock concerts, including a legendary performance by the Beatles on Sunday, August 15, 1965.

On June 5, 1987, Marvel staged the wedding of Spider-Man and Mary Jane Watson at the real world's Shea Stadium, just before the start of a game between the New York Mets and the Pittsburgh Pirates. In attendance at the wedding were Captain America; the Hulk; Firestar and Iceman, who were the costars of the animated TV series *Spider-Man and His Amazing Friends;* and perhaps inappropriately, Spider-Man's enemies Doctor Doom and the Green Goblin. The Marvel characters were all played by actors, except for the real Stan Lee, who presided over the ceremony. (Actually, in the comics, Peter Parker and Mary Jane were married on the steps of City Hall in Manhattan.)

In the comics, Shea Stadium was the site of Spider-Man's notorious battle against a clone of himself, created by the costumed villain the Jackal (*Amazing Spider-Man*, Vol. 1, #149,

October 1975). A bomb planted by the Jackal exploded, seemingly killing the clone. But years later, the clone, who called himself Ben Reilly, returned in the famous "Clone Saga." For a time Peter Parker thought he himself was the clone, and Reilly took over the role of Spider-Man, until the truth was finally revealed, Reilly perished, and Peter resumed his costumed identity.

The evil sorcerer Dr. Angst once captured Doctor Strange, the Defenders, and Howard the Duck and magically teleported them to Shea Stadium. There Howard managed to defeat Dr. Angst by wrapping him in Strange's cloak of levitation and knocking him out (*Marvel Treasury Edition* #12, 1976).

One might think that after their past misdeeds no one would ever again book the Ringmaster and his Circus of Crime in New York City. But the Circus gave a performance in Shea Stadium, where the Ringmaster once again hypnotized the audience in order to rob them. Daredevil turned up, battled the Circus, and thwarted the Ringmaster's scheme. However, a new member of the Circus, named Blackwing, escaped (*Daredevil*, vol. 1, #118, February 1975).

Blackwing was really Joseph Manfredi, the son of the Maggia crime lord Silvermane, who had taken control of the New York City operations of the subversive organization Hydra. Incredibly, Hydra had succeeded in building an entire underground headquarters beneath Shea Stadium. But SHIELD, under the direction of Nick Fury, invaded the clandestine base and easily put an end to Silvermane's faction of Hydra (*Daredevil,* vol. 1, #123, July 1975).

The Mets have started the construction of a new stadium, to be called Citi Field (after the Mets' sponsor Citigroup), in Shea Stadium's parking lot. When the new stadium opens in 2009, Shea Stadium will be dismantled. Whether Hydra will build a new headquarters under Citi Field remains to be seen. ✳

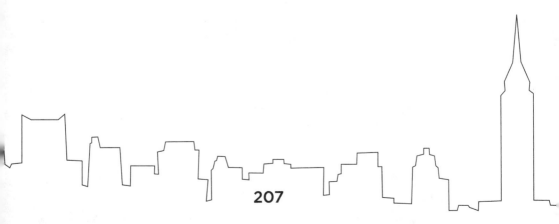

STATEN ISLAND

THE NEW YORK CITY borough with the smallest population is Staten Island, which, as its name suggests, is an island, separate from the rest of the city. That's lucky for Staten Island residents in the Marvel Universe, since the Super Villains who prowl the rest of the city almost never venture there.

The principal exception is Adrian Toomes, an elderly electronics engineer. Years ago he retired to his farm on Staten Island, where he perfected his invention: an electromagnetic harness that permitted whoever wore it to fly (*Amazing Spider-Man,* vol. 1, #240, May 1983). Using this device, Toomes became the costumed criminal known as the Vulture, one of Spider-Man's greatest enemies.

Perhaps more famous than Staten Island itself is the Staten Island ferry, which travels between lower Manhattan and Staten Island twenty-four hours a day. The scenic twenty-five-minute ride, which currently is free, makes the ferry a favorite with tourists and New Yorkers alike. Peter Parker and his girlfriend Debra Whitman once rode the ferry on a memorably romantic—if inexpensive—date (*Amazing Spider-Man,* vol. 1, #213, January 1981).

Through a strange accident, a fossil skeleton transformed into a living, flesh-and-blood pterodactyl, which attacked the

Staten Island ferry before it was killed (*Monsters on the Prowl* #15, February 1972).

Captain America and Spider-Man once blew up one of the ferries to destroy a monster from another dimension that had gotten aboard (*Marvel Team-Up,* vol. 1, #52, December 1976).

Notice that in neither case did the monster actually reach Staten Island, which remains a safety zone—for now—in Marvel's New York. ✳

STATEN ISLAND

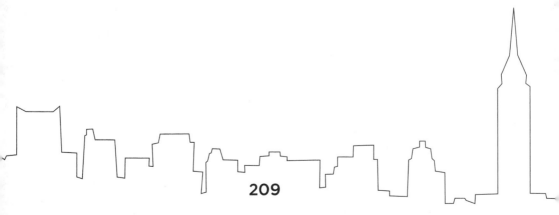

209

LONG ISLAND

THE BOROUGHS OF BROOKLYN and Queens are located on the west end of Long Island, the largest island in the United States (excluding Alaska and Hawaii). Beyond the city limits lie Nassau and Suffolk counties, suburban areas of Long Island with generally affluent populations.

Many Marvel characters were born on Long Island, including siblings Susan and Johnny Storm, who became the Fantastic Four's Invisible Woman and Human Torch. Their hometown was the fictional locale called Glenville, where they continued to live in the early days of their Super Hero careers (as shown in the Human Torch stories in *Strange Tales* in the 1960s).

When he was exposed as a mutant, teenager Bobby Drake was nearly lynched by a mob in his hometown of Port Washington, Long Island. Luckily, Professor Charles Xavier used his telepathic abilities to quiet the lynch mob and recruited Bobby to become Iceman of the X-Men (*X-Men* [first series] #44–46, May–July 1968).

Another member of the original X-Men, Warren Worthington III, alias the Angel, was born in the wealthy Long Island community of Centerport. Tony Stark, alias Iron Man, was also born on Long Island and grew up in a family mansion there.

Alison Blaire, the mutant pop singer called the Dazzler,

had more humble beginnings in a fictional Long Island suburb called Gardendale. Though born in Queens, Richard Rider, alias the Super Hero Nova, attended Harry S Truman High School in Hempstead, Long Island (*Nova,* vol. 1, #1, September 1976).

The Super Hero team known as the Defenders once had their headquarters out on Long Island at the Richmond Riding Academy, owned by Kyle Richmond, alias the Super Hero Nighthawk.

It's not just Super Heroes who lived on Long Island, however. The criminal genius known as the Wizard owns a Long Island mansion filled with advanced technology in which he once entrapped the Human Torch (*Strange Tales,* vol. 1, #102, November 1962). ✳

STARK INDUSTRIES/STARK INTERNATIONAL
Long Island

FOR MANY YEARS THE leading company designing and manufacturing advanced technology on Marvel-Earth was Stark Industries, which first appeared in *Tales of Suspense* #40 (April 1963). Founded by the late entrepreneur Howard Stark, the company achieved its height under the leadership of his son Anthony, a genius at technological innovation and invention.

Under Tony Stark's guidance, Stark Industries established branches all over the world, resulting in its being renamed Stark International (*Iron Man,* vol. 1, #73, March 1975).

But the company remained based in its original headquarters on Long Island, on the shores of Long Island Sound. The property covers two square miles and includes the administration building, research and development laboratories, and a factory complex. There is even a shipyard on Long Island Sound and an airfield. Transportation around the complex is provided by a monorail system. The environmentally aware Stark even built a solar-converter power plant to provide the entire complex with energy.

Stark Industries/International was famously protected by Tony Stark's "bodyguard," Iron Man, the Super Hero whose armored battlesuit Stark personally designed. The world was unaware that Stark himself was Iron Man. Numerous Marvel stories from the 1960s onward depict Iron Man battling Super Villains on the grounds of Stark Industries.

But where exactly on Long Island was the Stark Industries complex? Some early Iron Man stories indicate that Stark Industries was located in Flushing, a section of Queens. That would place Stark Industries within New York City. (Queens and Brooklyn are indeed technically located on Long Island.) However, far more Iron Man stories simply refer to Stark Industries or Stark International as being located on Long Island, implying that the site lay beyond these two outer boroughs.

During a period when he had lost control of his company, Tony Stark founded a consulting firm, Stark Solutions, which was originally based in a new skyscraper in Manhattan's "Silicon Alley," an area around the Flatiron Building where new companies dealing in personal-computer and internet technology had sprung up (*Iron Man,* vol. 3, #1–2, February–March 1998).

Eventually Stark regained control of his original company, which is today known once again as Stark Industries and is located on Long Island. Presumably it occupies the same site as the original Stark Industries.

Stark has recently built a Manhattan skyscraper, Stark Tower, which has become the new headquarters of the Avengers. *

STARK INDUSTRIES/STARK INTERNATIONAL

DAY TRIPS: THE X-MANSION AND MORE

MARVEL'S NEW YORK CITY is the nexus of Super Hero activity, but the action spills over into other locations in the so-called tristate area, comprising Connecticut, New Jersey, and New York State.

The most important Marvel-related site outside New York City is the Xavier Mansion (nicknamed the X-Mansion), the headquarters of the Marvel Universe's leading team of mutant Super Heroes, the uncanny X-Men.

The mansion is the ancestral home of the X-Men's founder, Professor Charles Xavier, and is located at 1407 Graymalkin Lane in the town of Salem Center in New York State's Westchester County. The mansion is three miles from the center of Salem Center, and forty miles from New York City. Xavier's

mansion is the largest building on his family estate, which stretches from Graymalkin Lane to Breakstone Lake.

The first thing that the tourist will want to know is how real this address is. Westchester County is certainly real. Located just north of New York City, it includes several cities, including New Rochelle, White Plains, and Yonkers, a large number of towns such as Mamaronek, North Salem, and Scarsdale, villages such as Tarrytown and Sleepy Hollow (site of Washington Irving's famous ghost story), and even smaller communities, known as hamlets, such as Chappaqua, the home of former president Bill Clinton.

One of the wealthiest counties in the United States, Westchester County contains such famous mansions as Kykuit, the home of the Rockefeller family, and the Gothic revival mansion Lyndhurst, both located in Tarrytown.

There is a real place called Salem Center, but it is only a small hamlet within the town of North Salem, in the northeast corner of Westchester County. Longtime X-Men writer Chris Claremont expanded Salem Center into an entire town in the Marvel Universe.

Real-world residents of North Salem include New York City mayor Michael Bloomberg, actor Paul Newman, and comedian David Letterman. Whether they are also the X-Men's neighbors in the Marvel Universe is unknown.

Both Graymalkin Lane and Breakstone Lake, on the opposite end of Xavier's property, are fictional.

The mansion was originally constructed in the eighteenth century by a Dutch ancestor of Xavier's, using stone from the edge of the aptly named Breakstone Lake. The mansion and the estate have belonged to Xavier's family for ten generations.

When Charles Xavier founded the X-Men, he was already a renowned authority on mutation, but he had not publicly revealed himself to be a mutant. Likewise, the original members of the X-Men—Angel, Beast, Cyclops, Iceman, and Marvel Girl—passed as ordinary human beings in their everyday identities. The general public's fear and suspicion of superhuman mutants was so strong that it would have been dangerous for them to do otherwise.

Therefore, Xavier opened Professor Xavier's School for Gifted Youngsters, based in his mansion. (The mansion and its school first appeared in *X-Men* [first series] #1, September 1963.) As far as the public was concerned, this was a highly exclusive private school, with only five students, whom Xavier provided with the equivalent of a high school and college education. Secretly, within the mansion Xavier trained his pupils in mastering their superhuman abilities and becoming skilled in combat.

In time Xavier's original pupils grew into adults, of course, and most of his new recruits into the X-Men, such as Storm and Wolverine, were already adults. Xavier therefore recruited a new class of superpowered adolescents, the New Mutants, who studied and trained at the mansion as well. They, too, inevitably grew older, and it became clear that the name School for Gifted Youngsters no longer applied. Hence, in *X-Men* (second series) #38 (November 1994), the school was renamed the Xavier Institute for Higher Learning. Hence, Xavier's veteran pupils could now be regarded as pursuing graduate studies.

Xavier purchased another private school, the Massachusetts Academy, located in the fictional town of Snow Valley in western Massachusetts' Berkshire Mountains. There he founded a new School for Gifted Youngsters, where headmasters Sean Cassidy (the Banshee, a former X-Men member) and Emma Frost (the White Queen) instructed yet another class of teenage mutants, known as Generation X. Eventually, however, this satellite institution was closed.

In recent years the world has learned that Charles Xavier is himself a mutant, and that his school is the headquarters for the X-Men. Xavier then vastly expanded the school, recruiting over a hundred teenage students, eventually even accepting some who were not mutants. Various senior members of the X-Men served as teachers at the school, as seen both in the comics and in the feature films.

Although the general public was long unaware that Xavier's school was a cover for the X-Men, many of the mutant team's enemies were well aware of the fact. Though the Xavier mansion had endured for two centuries before the founding of the X-Men, since then it has repeatedly been demolished and rebuilt. First it was wrecked by the alien Sidrian Hunters, and later the reconstructed mansion was blown up by Mr. Sinister. On each occasion the mansion was rebuilt in accordance with the original design.

However, after an impostor posing as Magneto recently blew up the mansion, Scott Summers (Cyclops) and Emma Frost decided to construct a much larger mansion on-site to accommodate the vastly expanded student body.

The exterior of the current X-Mansion follows the same architectural style as the original, but is appropriately shaped like an X.

The trademark feature of each previous version of the mansion was its central cupola, a small, ornamental domed tower atop the roof, which afforded a scenic view of the estate. The current X-Mansion instead has a much larger "observation tower" rising from the center of the X.

Visitors follow a driveway to the mansion's entrance courtyard, whose centerpiece is a statue of Phoenix, alias Jean Grey, one of the original X-Men. To the sides of the main entrance are wings that house the Xavier Institute's classrooms. Professor Xavier's office is on the top floor of the center of the *X*. The living room, dining room, and library are housed in this central part of the mansion. To the rear of the central portion of the complex is the school cafeteria. The remaining arms of the *X*, on either side of the cafeteria, lead to the boys' and girls' dormitories.

To the left of the building is the memorial garden, a version of which appears in the movie *X-Men: The Last Stand* (2006). To the right of the building is a hedge maze, in the tradition of similar mazes on various English estates. Directly behind the mansion are an outdoor basketball court and an Olympic-size swimming pool. It is only a short walk from there to Break-stone Lake. Stables and a boathouse are located elsewhere on the estate. The hangar for the X-Men's aircraft, such as the Blackbird or "X-Jet," lies underground beneath the basketball court.

As at Avengers Mansion, most of the training facilities and computer systems are located in basements and subbasements for security reasons.

The best-known room in the X-Mansion is the Danger Room, where the X-Men test their combat skills. The original Danger

Room included various hidden traps, conventional weaponry, and even robots. After Professor Xavier formed an alliance with Princess Lilandra of the alien Shi'ar, he incorporated Shi'ar technology that enabled him to create solid holographic menaces and settings for the X-Men's training exercises. In *X-Men: The Last Stand*, for example, the Danger Room conjures up holograms of a gigantic Sentinel robot and a war-torn cityscape. In the comics, the Shi'ar-based Danger Room technology proved to be sentient and escaped, and so the X-Men have gone back to more conventional training exercises in the Danger Room.

Professor Xavier invented a computer system called Cerebro, which amplifies his mental powers to better enable him to detect the location of superhuman mutants. In the comics the most recent version of this system is called Cerebra, but in the movies it is still known as Cerebro. In both the comics and the movies, the system is housed in the X-Mansion basement.

The building used for the exterior shots of the Xavier mansion in the three *X-Men* movies is not located in Westchester County, or even in the United States. However, it is indeed a school. The movies' X-Mansion is really Hatley Castle, on Vancouver Island, off British Columbia in Canada. Completed in 1908, the castle was originally the home of James Dunsmuir, the wealthy heir to a coal business who became premier of British Columbia. The castle is now the main administration building for Royal Roads University.

Anyone looking for the X-Mansion in the alternate continuity of Marvel's Ultimate X-Men would search in vain, since its location is shielded by the holographic projection of a Jehovah's Witnesses headquarters!

As for Marvel's fictional version of Salem Center, the comics have revealed almost nothing about the town apart from the Xavier estate. However, Xavier Institute students' and teachers' favorite local hangout is Harry's Hideaway, a tavern and restaurant owned and operated by Harry Morrel, a man with a mysterious past.

Also in Westchester County, somewhere to the southwest of Salem Center, is the fictional Ravencroft Asylum for the

Criminally Insane, which has facilities for imprisoning superhuman criminals. Spider-Man's foes the Chameleon and Carrion have each been incarcerated here. The former director of the Ravencroft Asylum bore the appropriate name of Dr. Ashley Kafka. She was succeeded by the superhumanly powerful psychologist Dr. Leonard "Doc" Samson.

Much farther upstate, amid the scenic Adirondack Mountains, are several other important fictional locales in Marvel history. (The Adirondack Mountains are located within the 6.1 million acres that make up Adirondack Park, the largest park in the continental United States.)

First is Whisper Hill, the eerie, isolated site of the large Victorian house in which the witch Agatha Harkness made her home (first seen in *Fantastic Four* #94, January 1970). Reed Richards of the Fantastic Four chose Harkness to be the nanny for his son Franklin, hoping that her supernatural powers would protect him from the team's enemies.

North of Whisper Hill is the European-style castle in the Adirondacks that Doctor Doom has sometimes used as his American base of operations. Here he housed the time machine that he used in his first encounter with the Fantastic Four (*Fantastic Four* #5, July 1962). Captain America and the Avengers later visited the castle to use the time machine themselves (*Avengers* #56, September 1968).

To the west, toward Lake Ontario, is the headquarters of Project: Pegasus, a scientific research center, which is run by the federal government's Department of Energy, and which specializes in research into alternative energy sources. *Pegasus* is an acronym for Potential Energy Group/Alternate Sources/ United States. Introduced in *Marvel Two-in-One* #42 (August 1978), the Project headquarters stands on the fictional Mount Athena in the Adirondacks. Among the energy sources that Project: Pegasus scientists have studied are superpowered criminals, some of whom have temporarily been incarcerated there. The Squadron Supreme, a Super Hero team from a parallel Earth, resided in Project: Pegasus during an extended stay on Marvel-Earth.

Northwest of Project: Pegasus, near Lake Ontario, is the Serpent Citadel, the former base used by the Serpent Society, an organization of costumed criminals with snake motifs, such as Thor's foe the Cobra. The Citadel building was previously used as an insane asylum.

Elsewhere in the Adirondacks is the hidden mountain base that Larry Trask used as a base for the Sentinels, the mutant-hunting robots invented by his father, Dr. Bolivar Trask (*X-Men* [first series] #57–59, June–August 1969). Years later, the Super Hero team X-Force took over this abandoned base.

Count Luchino Nefaria, the Italian aristocrat who was a

leader of the Italian crime syndicate called the Maggia, had his ancestral castle disassembled stone by stone and rebuilt in New Jersey, where he had his first confrontation with the Avengers (*Avengers*, vol. 1, #13, February 1965). To shield his criminal activities, Nefaria opened the castle to tours by the public, and presumably it continues to be a tourist attraction in Marvel's New Jersey.

Some Super Heroes have made their homes in New Jersey, close enough to easily commute to New York City, but far enough away to experience relative peace and quiet. Heiress Janet van Dyne, who, as the Super Heroine called the Wasp was a cofounder of the Avengers, owns a large house, complete with swimming pool, in Cresskill, New Jersey (*Avengers*, vol. 1, #274, December 1986). When they were married, two other Avengers, the Vision and the Scarlet Witch, bought a home in the small, peaceful town of Leonia, New Jersey (*The Vision and the*

Scarlet Witch miniseries, 1985–86). Both towns are quite real and accessible by mass transit.

Reed and Susan Richards experimented with maintaining secret identities as "the Benjamins" in the small, fictional town of Belle Port, Connecticut. The other inhabitants of this idyllic spot bear striking resemblances to characters from classic newspaper comic strips, as shown in *Fantastic Four,* vol. 1, #276 (March 1985).

In the Marvel Universe, the real-life city of Stamford, Connecticut, in easy commuting distance of New York, was the site of a disaster with far-reaching repercussions. The Super Villain Nitro was battling the young Super Heroes called the New Warriors in Stamford when he blew himself up. Nitro's superpowers enabled him to reassemble his body, but the tremendous force of the detonation killed not only most of the New Warriors, but also sixty schoolchildren in the vicinity. This massacre gave further impetus to the movement to force all Super Heroes to register with the federal government, leading to the "civil war" among the Marvel heroes (*Civil War* #1–6, 2006–7). ✳

DAY TRIPS: THE X-MANSION AND MORE

THE SPIDER-MAN TOUR

PERHAPS NO MARVEL SUPER HERO is as closely identified with New York City as Spider-Man. A tourist in New York City can easily visit many of the major sites of importance in Spider-Man's history, both in the comics and on-screen, within a single day exploring Manhattan and Queens. Here, for your entertainment and convenience, are a selection of sites listed in one place.

MANHATTAN

Morningside Heights

COLUMBIA UNIVERSITY

Movies: In the first *Spider-Man* movie, Peter Parker is bitten by a genetically modified spider at Columbia. By *Spider-Man 2*, Peter has become a student at Columbia College, taught by Dr. Curt Connors.

RIVERSIDE CHURCH

490 Riverside Drive, between West 120th and 122nd Streets
Movies: This is where Mary Jane Watson nearly married John Jameson in *Spider-Man 2*.

BEDFORD TOWERS

Comics: After Peter Parker married Mary Jane Watson, they moved into a condo in the luxurious Bedford Towers on the Upper West Side. Peter couldn't afford it, but Mary Jane could, since she was at the height of her modeling career. But they didn't stay there long. The building's owner, Jonathan Caesar, enraged that Mary Jane had spurned him, evicted the Parkers at Christmastime in *Amazing Spider-Man,* vol. 1, #314 (April 1989).

AMERICAN MUSEUM OF NATURAL HISTORY

Movies: In *Spider-Man 2,* Peter Parker attends the "Science Library Benefit" at the museum's Rose Center for Earth and Space, where Mary Jane Watson and John Jameson announce their engagement.

Central Park

Movies: Under threat from Harry Osborn, Mary Jane Watson breaks off her relationship with Peter Parker atop a bridge in Central Park in *Spider-Man 3.*

MANHATTAN

Upper East Side

J. JONAH JAMESON'S PENTHOUSE
Park Avenue in the Lower East Seventies

Comics: This is where *Daily Bugle* publisher J. Jonah Jameson lives with his second wife, Dr. Marla Madison Jameson.

NORMAN OSBORN'S PENTHOUSE
Park Avenue in the Upper East Sixties

Comics: Home of Norman Osborn, the original Green Goblin.

Midtown

QUEENSBORO BRIDGE
Off East Fifty-ninth Street

ROOSEVELT ISLAND
Movies: Spider-Man saves Mary Jane and a tramload of passengers in the first *Spider-Man* movie, as New Yorkers on the bridge cheer him on. Later, Spider-Man battles the Goblin to the death on Roosevelt Island.

THE DAILY GLOBE BUILDING
Third Avenue near East Fifty-fourth Street

Comics: *The Daily Globe,* another New York tabloid newspaper, is the longtime rival of J. Jonah Jameson's *Daily Bugle.*

TUDOR CITY
Fortieth to Forty-third Streets between First and Second Avenues

Movies: This residential complex includes the apartment where Norman Osborn lives in the first movie, and his son Harry in the second and third films.

FIFTY-FOURTH STREET AND AVENUE OF THE AMERICAS (SIXTH AVENUE)

Movies: The web-slinger saves Gwen Stacy when she falls from an office building at this site in *Spider-Man 3.*

ROCKEFELLER CENTER

Movies: After saving Mary Jane Watson's life in the first movie, Spider-Man leaves her in a roof garden atop one of the buildings in Rockefeller Center.

TIMES SQUARE

Movies: Spider-Man battles the Green Goblin during a festival held in Times Square in the first movie. Peter Parker meets Stan Lee in Times Square in *Spider-Man 3.*

BROADHURST THEATER
235 West Forty-fourth Street

Movies: Mary Jane performs in a Broadway musical here in *Spider-Man 3.*

MADAME WEB'S APARTMENT
East Forties

Comics: At her apartment the blind Madame Web used her mental powers to predict the future, as first shown in *Amazing Spider-Man*, vol. 1, #210 (November 1980).

NEW YORK PUBLIC LIBRARY/HUMANITIES AND SOCIAL SCIENCES LIBRARY
Fifth Avenue and Forty-second Street

Movies: Peter Parker's uncle Ben is shot and killed across Fifth Avenue from the library in *Spider-Man*.

DAILY BUGLE BUILDING
East Thirty-ninth Street and Second Avenue

Comics: Site of the editorial offices for J. Jonah Jameson's tabloid newspaper, where Peter Parker works as a freelance photographer.

CURT CONNORS'S APARTMENT
East Forties

Comics: Home of the brilliant, one-armed biochemist who has repeatedly transformed into the Lizard, a superstrong reptile with human intelligence.

FISK TOWERS
East Thirties

Comics: This is the headquarters for Wilson Fisk, the Kingpin of Crime, who long dominated organized crime in New York City. The Kingpin first clashed with Spider-Man in *Amazing Spider-Man* #50 (July 1987). Publicly, Fisk claimed to be an honest businessman or, as he put it, a humble "dealer in spices."

EMPIRE STATE BUILDING

Movies: The Empire State Building is prominently shown on several occasions in the first three *Spider-Man* movies.

DAILY BUGLE OFFICES
Flatiron Building, Twenty-third Street

Movies: Site of the editorial offices of J. Jonah Jameson's tabloid newspaper in the *Spider-Man* movies.

MADISON SQUARE PARK

Movies: Fleeing her wedding to John Jameson, Mary Jane runs across Madison Square Park in *Spider-Man 2* to reach Peter Parker's apartment.

MANHATTAN

Greenwich Village

EMPIRE STATE UNIVERSITY

Comics: Peter Parker did both his undergraduate and graduate studies at this fictional New York campus based on New York University, which surrounds Washington Square Park.

JOE'S PIZZA (NOW CLOSED)

233 Bleecker Street at Carmine Street

Movies: Peter Parker works here as a pizza delivery boy at the start of *Spider-Man 2*.

East Village

ANTHOLOGY FILM ARCHIVES

32 Second Avenue (at Second Street)

Movies: This movie theater was used in *Spider-Man 2* as Doctor Octopus's home and laboratory.

ASTOR PLACE

Lafayette Street

Movies: Doctor Octopus hurls a car through the window of a restaurant in Astor Place in *Spider-Man 2*, nearly killing Peter Parker and Mary Jane Watson.

650 SPRING STREET

Movies: The site of the bank robbed by Doctor Octopus in *Spider-Man 2*.

MOONDANCE DINER

80 Sixth Avenue at Grand Street

Movies: Mary Jane works here as a waitress in the first *Spider-Man* film.

Lower East Side

187 CHRYSTIE STREET

Movies: This building is used for the exterior shot of Peter Parker's apartment house in *Spider-Man 2* and *3*.

East River

MASTER PLANNER'S UNDERSEA BASE

Comics: In *Amazing Spider-Man* #32–33 (January–February 1966), Doctor Octopus, calling himself the Master Planner, operates a secret base of operations beneath the East River. In one of the most famous sequences in his history, Spider-Man is pinned beneath tons of metal as the base begins to collapse, but with heroic effort succeeds in throwing the massive weight from his shoulders.

BROOKLYN BRIDGE

Comics: In *Amazing Spider-Man* #121 (May 1973), the Green Goblin murders Peter Parker's girlfriend Gwen Stacy by throwing her off the top of the Brooklyn Bridge.

Lower Manhattan

CITY HALL

City Hall Park, Broadway at Park Row

Comics: Peter Parker married Mary Jane Watson in front of City Hall in *Amazing Spider-Man Annual* #21 (1987).
Movies: After rescuing her from Doctor Octopus in *Spider-Man 2*, Spider-Man leaves Aunt May safely in City Hall Park.

WALL STREET

Movies: In *Spider-Man 3*, Gwen Stacy hosts the city's celebration of their "friendly neighborhood Spider-Man" in the Wall Street area.

QUEENS

Forest Hills

MAY PARKER'S HOUSE

Comics: 20 Ingram Street in Forest Hills Gardens.

MAY PARKER'S HOUSE

Movies: Sixty-ninth Road between Metropolitan Avenue and Sybilla Street.

MIDTOWN HIGH SCHOOL

Comics and movies: The school that Peter Parker attended is presumably based on the actual Forest Hills High School at 67-01 110th Street.

Woodside

Movies: The opening sequence in the first *Spider-Man,* in which Peter Parker runs down the street to catch the school bus, was supposedly set in Forest Hills. However, it was actually filmed on Queens Boulevard at Forty-forth Street in another Queens neighborhood, Woodside. ✳

A NOTE ON GETTING AROUND NEW YORK

NEW YORK CITY IS one of the world's most walkable cities, and we hope that by arranging this guide by neigborhood, we have encouraged you to devise your own walking tours that will take you past multiple sites of Marvel importance. But keep in mind that New York also boasts a comprehensive mass-transportation system of subways, buses, commuter trains, and ferries. All New York City sites listed in this guide (the real-world ones, at least!) are easily accessible using various mass-transit options. Please visit www.mta.info for useful information on the New York City transit system. ✳

PHOTOGRAPHY CREDITS